I0048519

Real Estate Investing For Women

Expert Conversations to Increase Wealth
and Happiness the Blissful Way

Moneeka Sawyer

Real Estate Investing For Women: Expert Conversations to Increase Wealth and Happiness the Blissful Way

Copyright © 2020 by Moneeka Sawyer
www.Blissfulinvestor.com

Published by RHG Media Productions, 25495 Southwick Drive #103, Hayward, CA 94544.
ISBN 978-1-088-16850-9

All rights reserved. No part of this publication may be reproduced, distributed, or transmitted in any form or by any means, including photocopying, recording, or other electronic or mechanical methods, without prior written permission of the publisher, except in the case of brief quotations embodied in critical reviews and certain other noncommercial uses permitted by copyright law.

Printed in the United State of America.

CONTENTS

BLISSFUL WEALTH
WITH MONEEKA SAWYER

In 2008, I bought the home of my dreams. I'd worked hard for years building my net worth, and I felt like now I could splurge and get myself the home I really wanted. I spent a million dollars on it. It was like I had just gotten my Barbie dream house!

Then SNAP! Just like that, the market tanked, and within 6 months I'd lost more than 50% of the value of my home.

I would sit at my computer each morning and look up my home value on Zillow, and each day I would watch the price go down. I felt a deep gnawing hole in the pit of my belly that I couldn't shake. Suddenly my dream had become my nightmare.

I remember lying in the fetal position in bed for several days. I was so scared. Was the bank going to call my loan because we were so underwater? Would I be homeless? But my biggest fear was my husband. We'd bought this place for me, against his better judgment, and now look at what happened. I knew he loved me, but was this unforgivable? I felt like I didn't have any choices. What was going to happen to me?

How had this happened to me? Successful real estate investor, rational businesswoman . . . How had I not seen this coming?

As I lay there in bed one morning, I heard my dad's voice in my head. I remembered an evening long ago when my dad told me about an article he'd read by Warren Buffett. He said, "If you can't control your emotions, you can't control your money."

In that moment, I sat up and rubbed my eyes. This was my salvation. I knew how to manage my emotions. This was the ultimate test. Could I do it in these desperate times?

I thought to myself, "Moneeka, you don't lose money until you sell." We still loved living in this home; all I needed to do was ride out this storm in the market. I could make that choice!

Every day the people around me were saying things like "I've lost my entire life savings." "I'm drowning paying a mortgage that is higher than the value of my house." "What am I going to do? I'm going to lose everything."

If I tried gently to warn them against making emotional decisions, they exclaimed, "I'm not making an emotional decision! I'm totally in control!"

For me, I decided to try to stay rational and not freak out in the situation.

Then, I got news that my husband needed to get a new job and we had to move. I could have done what others had done in this situation: choose to sell this anchor around my neck and cut my losses. Instead, I looked at it rationally. All I had to do was hold on and wait.

So, I chose to rent out my dream home, and because my husband had taken a pay cut, we had to move into a little dump we could afford in our new area. Even though I was heartbroken having to live in that place, I fixed it up so it was livable and went on with my life.

Fast-forward nine years. The market had recovered, and we were able to move back to my dream home. By then, the dump had appreciated $500,000. And surprisingly, my dream home had recovered and gone up an additional $500,000. Somehow, through the nightmare that was the 2008 economic crash, even though I had bought at the top of the market, I had made $1,000,000!

Through this experience I learned a lot. First, I strengthened my own strategies to lower stress and create what I call Bliss: a deep sense of joy and contentment, and the confidence that you can handle anything that comes your way. It is emotional mastery and emotional resilience.

Second, I learned a lot about human behavior. I watched so many people around me give up their homes to foreclosure, uproot their lives, file for bankruptcy, and suffer a lot. Certainly, there were many people who didn't have any other choices during that crazy time. But many people didn't have to go through all that pain. And I realized no one was telling them what their options were.

That was the beginning of my journey to where I am now, educating people on how to build wealth with real estate. This all started because I wanted just to educate people on how not to suffer. How to stay emotionally balanced enough to look at their options and make decisions that serve them better. We can't change or control the circumstances that happen in the world; sometimes life does get difficult, but we do have control over how we choose to respond. We can make choices that will keep us closer to our bliss.

As my journey has expanded, I've learned so much more. Through my radio show and podcast, Real Estate Investing for Women, I get to talk to experts more successful than me in their fields. It's exhilarating and has been such a blessing in my life and to my bank account. That's why I decided to put together this book. I wanted to compile the best advice from my podcast so investors could have the information at their fingertips. I invited my most popular guests on the show to join me in this project. The end result is this truly amazing compilation of wisdom, strategies, and wealth-building techniques. I'm so honored to be in such powerful company, and I'm delighted to bring all this knowledge, insight, and understanding to you.

I hope you enjoy it. As you know, educating yourself is very important for your success, but nothing happens until you actually start acting on what you learn. So, enjoy this book. Absorb everything it has to offer you. Allow it to inspire, educate, and uplift you. Then go out there, take action, and create the life your heart deeply desires

The Mindset and Heartset of Blissful Wealth

Build the foundation inside of you to create blissful wealth successfully.

FINDING SUCCESS THROUGH OPTIMISM
AND BEING GOOD TO OTHERS
WITH LEEZA GIBBONS

Moneeka: Today I am delighted to welcome our guest, Leeza Gibbons! Leeza is a TV and radio host, author, speaker, philanthropist, caregiver, advocate, wife, and mom. She is best known as a co-host for Entertainment Tonight as well as for having her own syndicated daytime talk show, Leeza.

She received the 1998 Horizon Award from the United States Congress. The Horizon Award is a special recognition from the joint leadership of the United States Congress and the Congressional Award Board of Directors to individuals from the private sector who have contributed to expanding opportunities for all Americans through their own personal contributions and who have set exceptional examples for young people through their success in life.

In 2013, Leeza's book Take 2 became a New York Times bestseller and she won the Daytime Emmy for outstanding host for the PBS show My Generation.

On February 16th, 2015, Leeza was named the winner of Celebrity Apprentice, having raised $714,000 for her personal charity, Leeza's Care Connection.

Leeza believes in second chances, spreading kindness, and imagining a world without Alzheimer's.

Hi Leeza, welcome to the show. How are you?

Leeza: I'm doing great, and it's really great to talk to you. It's good to see you again.

Moneeka: I can't believe this happened, but Leeza and I happened to meet at a seminar about a month ago, and I just couldn't resist asking her to be on the show. She has some amazing stories that you ladies will love hearing. Thank you for spending this time with us, Leeza!

Leeza: It's funny because when we met, it was clear that we share a lot of the same sort of life philosophies and our optics on business are very much the same. I just applaud the work that you do with your podcast.

Moneeka: Thank you, Leeza. That's so flattering. I can't wait to talk about the work that you're doing in the world. I wanted to start today's conversation with your story about your mentors and your Barbie doll. Do you mind sharing that? It is so funny.

Leeza: When I was a child growing up in this small town in South Carolina—I don't have any idea what a therapist would say about this—but I didn't play house a lot. I didn't have doll babies that I was diapering and all the rest. But I did love to play and weave some very big dreams with my Barbie dolls.

I called Barbie my first feminist friend because with Barbie, I could envision that I really did rule the world. All of my Barbies were reporters. That was my dream. I thought, "Okay, I'm going to get in the broadcast business. I just want to be a storyteller." Barbie ran the world and she had businesses also, and it was really a great way for me to imagine what was possible.

I think in life we really do become how we self-identify. I mean, if you're an athlete, then you eat like an athlete, you create strength like an athlete, and you're disciplined like an athlete. If you say you're an optimist, then you look for good outcomes and you put that frame on everything. It was really a very fertile dream ground for me.

Moneeka: I love that term dream ground! And your head Barbie was named Barbara Walters? Is that true?

Leeza: Yes.

Moneeka: "Barbie Walters!"

Leeza: The most successful news women of the time were Barbara Walters and Nancy Dickerson. Barbara Walters was my head Barbie in charge.

It's funny because I have a younger sister and she would always say, "Well, I want to play, I want to play. What can I be? What can I be?" Well, I started out young being a control enthusiast because I thought, "Well, I like that better than not being in control."

So, I said to my kid sister, "Fine, you can play with me. That's fine. You be my assistant Barbie." She was quite fine with that.

Moneeka: That's totally awesome. Then when you got into the industry as a journalist, tell us a little bit about that journey and some of your mentors and how that worked. Because I think we don't always really understand that it's a journey. We see very successful people like you or others and we think, "Oh, they just got there." But it's a journey, and we all have to start somewhere. So, could you tell us a little bit about your journey?

Leeza: Sure, and we also have started to reward more and more impatience and that "Don't have a plan B" philosophy. All of that is great to fuel your dream, but it can also create this sort of unreal bubble of competition. And I think that if you stay in your lane and work your dream and have your side hustle, and whatever else you have to have to get there, then you're right on time.

Whenever you arrive, you're right on time.

The danger comes when we look to our left, we look to our right, we see the other horses racing beside us, and we feel competitive. We forget that in many cases, we're better just to not worry about how green their grass is, to just be so busy tending to our own garden that we don't even notice theirs. When we compare ourselves to others, it really does strip the joy out of life.

When you have all the places that we do to create whatever personal brand of ourselves that we want, sometimes we lose track of the authenticity. And the universal authentic experience is what you said Moneeka; it's the journey. It's what your mother always told you and what your instructors and the people that influenced your life always told you that the entire thing is learning - that's it. It is the journey. You have to find the joy in being on that path.

Moneeka: We all have heard the stories of people that became millionaires through winning the lottery or whatever. They get all pumped up, it's really exciting. Then within five years, they've lost everything. Part of that really speaks to that piece about the journey. We grow step by step into who we're supposed to be. If all of a sudden we're elevated to a particular place and we're not ready to be there, we're not able to be there successfully.

if you go through the journey and you learn and you grow and you become wealthy through the journey, when you're there, you can do so much more from that place and you can stay there as opposed to having been thrown there and then you lose all that wealth.

Leeza: I think being thrown off our equilibrium is a lot of what you're talking about. That has to do with work. They always say you get the life that you think you deserve. You make the money you think you deserve. You have the love that you think you deserve. I believe that there is a lot of validity to those statements. What makes us think that we deserve it? Well, we only respect ourselves when we do something that we find worthy. Something that we find hard for us.

So, it may be hard for somebody listening to us right now to ask for a raise. It may be hard to let go of a toxic relationship. Whatever the thing is that's hard, that's how you gain your self-respect. When you've done that enough through your journey, that's when you can be very secure that the success is yours to take, the money is yours, and the abundance is yours to have and to really own. That's when it's not fleeting and it doesn't fall through your fingers.

I think the problem with winning the lottery or getting some kind of instant fix is we haven't had time to do the kind of emotional work and build our own identities up to become a person who's worthy of that.

Moneeka: Yes, absolutely. I've had many clients come to me and say, "Moneeka, I want to be a millionaire in real estate." And my thing is, well, you need to be a thousand-aire first. You need to be a ten-thousand-aire first. You have to step into it a little bit at a time, get better and better and better at being perfectly you, and step into being bigger and bigger.

Leeza: I remember the first time I said that I wanted to be a millionaire. When I was in school and my head Barbie, Barbara Walters, became the first female network anchor of the Nightly News. The headline was that she was making a million dollars. That was more money than the guy! I thought that was the greatest thing of all time.

I went back to my little college freshman Broadcasting 101 class and I said, "Did you read that? Did you see that? Barbara Walters is making a million dollars in the broadcast business. That's what I'm going to do. I'm going to make a million dollars."

They laughed and laughed and laughed. They said, "Leeza, you're from Irmo, South Carolina. You're not going to make a million dollars. You're not even going to get out of town."

THE MINDSET AND HEARTSET OF BLISSFUL WEALTH | 15

That's when my mother was very helpful and said to me, "Stick with your vision, work your plan. Go out there and work your dream every day. Don't let someone else take that away." We give people permission to erode what we think is possible in our own lives. My mom really helped me stay on track.

When I started my career, I wrote a fan letter to Barbara Walters. I had watched an interview that she had done and I told her how great I thought she was. When she actually returned the letter, it was such an inspiration. Those little things (which was actually a very big thing) really kept me on track.

That's why I think that whatever successes we have in life from whatever platforms we happen to be on, it's always worth the time to reach out our hands and lift someone else along the journey. We may not think that we're the sage at the top of the mountain, and we may, in fact, not be that at all. But to someone, we've got something that they need to hear, and we don't always know what that something is unless we make ourselves an open vessel for it.

Moneeka: Thank you so much for that. I just think about so many people I admire, what if they had given up? What if they had listened to those people who said, "You're never even going to get out of town. You're never going to do that"? What if they had given up?

Leeza: A lot of people do. Although, I think that temporarily getting off the path is an opportunity to reaffirm where you don't want to be. To get where you're going, you have to be really sure of where you don't want to be anymore. That's what happens when we fall off the path.

I'm sort of an easy target to make fun of for my optimism. But I think that it doesn't mean that I am naïve, and it doesn't mean that I'm Pollyanna. Real optimists, people who are fiercely optimistic, have a mental competence. It's a skill set that anybody can develop. It's the thing you have that allows you to rebound and recover more quickly. I call this the "Tigger Effect." You know how Tigger would always just bounce around from one thing to the next? He was just a party all by himself.

If you think like that, just having that incredible ability to bounce back and fight back from anything, that's all it means to be an optimist. Luckily, we're all going to fail and we're all going to have challenges. We're all going to get off the path. That's when we engage this mental competency to be optimistic so that we get back on the path and we get to where we are going, instead of being derailed. We get to where we're going having strengthened that bounce-back muscle.

Moneeka: That's actually where our conversation originally started. I wrote the book Choose Bliss, which is about mastering your emotions, creating emotional resilience, and creating what I call the "bliss equilibrium," which is that place of optimism, joy, contentment, and the confidence that no matter what's going on, you can handle it. Life can't send you anything that you can't handle. That's how I'm defining bliss. It's also how you express optimism, and I love the parallels with that.

Leeza: I do, too. I think that as it relates to business, when you are offering your gifts, talents, and service to the world, that feeds back to you in the form of bliss. It gives you an invisible barrier of protection against the toxicity and the negativity that's out there so you can stay on your path.

There's a reason why cream separates and rises to the top. It's not for everybody to want the same thing. If you are separated from whatever pack it is that you find in your particular environment, and if you've self-identified as the cream, then it might be a little bit lonely, and that's by design. That means that you may need to look for other sources of inspiration.

I think that as women, and particularly women in business, it's so important that we recognize that we've become like the five people we spend the most time with. So, really edit that list carefully. Not to exclude people and dismiss them from your life, but just to release those relationships with love and no judgment, but knowing what's right for you.

It's just scientifically impossible not to become like those with whom we surround ourselves. I think that we have innate gifts and talents as women to work collaboratively, and we're nurturers by nature. So we must be able to offer that and know that when one woman succeeds, that takes nothing away from us. That just means that the whole ocean is getting bigger and that all the boats are rising up together. When watching her success we can think, "Great for her. Look at that. That happened. That means it's better for me." Not that it's taking something away from me.

I say girls compete, but women empower.

I think that real women, and especially real women leaders, are demonstrating that point of view more and more every day.

Moneeka: I totally agree. And you mentioned when we were having lunch an analogy about how women were like sequoias. How with the sequoia trees, their roots don't go deep. They go wide and then they tangle up with each other to hold each other up.

That's how we are as women. If we allow ourselves the opportunity to grow wide and reach for one another, we can wind our fingers together and hold each other up and make the world a better place for all of us as women. But also for the men and the children and the animals and everybody.

Leeza: It's true. It's really true. I do love that visual because you think about how impossibly big the sequoia is, and the girth and the weight and just the massiveness. But it only is possible for that tree to stand tall, as you say, because of the support system. The support system is that outreach and wrapping themselves around other trees. I do really believe that that's a great kind of mental reset for us, to recognize that we really are stronger together.

I think that in our political environment today, it's very easy for us to think that we don't have a voice or that we're just living in this kind of negative cesspool on both sides. That we are so divided. I believe that that's where women are uniquely qualified to point out the things that don't divide us. That's one of them. That we really are stronger together.

Moneeka: One of the things that really, really warmed my soul when we were having our conversation was when we started talking about our heart work. One of the things that I love about being successful as a woman, and being wealthy as a woman, is that it opens up opportunities for us to create so much more in the world. It allows us to make such a bigger impact and to do really, really good things.

I know a lot of people who listen to my podcast feel uncomfortable talking about and thinking about money. But if you think about it as an opportunity, or another way for you to do good in the world, then you do want to go after it more. One of the things that you and I really connected on is that view that money allows us to do so much good in the world.

So, I am wondering if you would tell us about what you're doing in the world with your organization.

Leeza: That's really nice, Moneeka. Thank you for asking. Since money is our currency of exchange, I do think that we need to look at how we leverage it and what it represents, and what opportunities it opens for us. Seeking financial abundance really does seem to make women uncomfortable. The sooner that you can actually own bringing in money, the sooner you will actually be able to create your bigger impact in the world. I used to have a mantra, "money flows to me easily." It shifted the energy in my life, and it can do the same for you.

For me, my heart work wasn't so much related to having a base of financial independence. Being financially independent was lovely and really helped me offer what I needed to offer, and wanted to offer, to my mom, who had Alzheimer's disease. It allowed me to ask, even through this place of limitation and fear and frustration, what do my family and I wish? It allowed me the freedom to consider what would have made this situation better for us? What would have helped us through it better? Instead of stumbling along, feeling so inadequate, feeling so guilty. Feeling just so ineffective at being able to help my mom who died of this disease that also took her mom. What could we have used as help? You know, every 65 seconds someone else is getting Alzheimer's disease.

That's what caused me to create what we now call Leeza's Care Connection, which really was just a manifestation of how do I make a "womb room?" A place that feels so safe, where we can help people find resources that they need and connect with other people.

We started this conversation by talking about the journey and the path and how we can connect other people on the path. That's what we've done. We've looked at the family care partners. There are millions of them out there, and they do something that can feel very lonely. It affects and impacts them so greatly that compassion fatigue assaults their body, and they often get sicker than the ones for whom they are caring.

So, it became the most inspiring, nourishing work that I've ever been able to do. To learn from the great resilience of all those people who were on that path and to put them together to offer support, resources, compassion, and connection based on a deep understanding of what they are going through. It's been really amazing.

Moneeka: In my book Choose Bliss, I wrote a chapter on the bliss of helping others. There's actually something called "the giver's high." When you're out there and you do good things for people, it boosts you up. It makes you feel better, it releases chemicals in your body. For women, it really connects us to that compassionate piece of ourselves.

When we're talking about giving to others, it's not just giving a lot of money or starting an organization. It can be as simple as giving a smile.

But what you remind us of is that there are also so many people out there giving so much of themselves that they get depleted. An organization like yours that really helps the caregivers remain human, remain compassionate for themselves, and is really such a big deal. Thank you so much for that work.

Leeza: It is a big deal. I appreciate that encouragement. It is a really big deal. Because if caregivers don't take care of themselves, if they don't get the support they need, then they're not present for work, they're not present for their children, they're depleted emotionally, spiritually, financially, and in every other way. They empty out completely.

So, job number one is to take your oxygen first and to make sure that you're not pouring from an empty vessel. Unfortunately, we're kind of good at pouring from an empty vessel. But, when you embrace self-care, when you can say, "I deserve money, I deserve to care for myself," that's when you get that self-respect.

When we talk about doing something hard, we often cringe. It's so worth pursuing because when you get there, then you can really own who you are. You can confidently ask yourself "How can I take better care of myself so that I can give more? How can I make more money in the world so that I can open more doors to spread my message, to offer my services, my talents (and whatever you choose to do with your money)?"

People may think, "Well, I just want to serve those underprivileged people." Great. But you can never be poor enough to offer them the greatest service. Instead, why not go in pursuit of either financial remuneration or some other reward? Then you can leverage that in the world to open up more doors to do more good. This is where, as you say so correctly, you'll find your bliss.

Moneeka: That is so true. Leeza, could you tell my listeners the website of your organization so that they can check it out if they are interested?

Leeza: Yes, of course. Thank you for that. It's **LeezasCareConnection. org**. We have physical locations, but we also would love to help you virtually. We can help connect you with some of our resource specialists and just be a voice to say, "We get it, we get you. We know what you're about."

Moneeka: Thank you, Leeza. This is so amazing. I have to say my little sister is the caretaker for my parents, and I do see her lose herself sometimes. What you are doing is just incredibly important. Thank you.

Leeza: Thank you for that, and a lot of strength to your sister and huge props.

Moneeka: I will tell her. So, Leeza, before we sign off, could you tell my audience one super tip on being successful?

Leeza: I find that most of my inspiration and my core tips really did come from my mom around our kitchen table. Mom used to always tell me, "Show up, do your best, let go of the rest." Those are three separate points that are very powerful each unto themselves.

Show up for your family, for yourself, for your beliefs, for your personal identity—show up. Those are the people that get ahead. It's not the ones with the highest IQ or the best connections. It's the ones who show up consistently.

Do your best—what a simple piece of advice. That will always set you up for the next moment.

Then "let go of the rest" is the piece that I think is the hardest to follow. Once you've been in that situation and you've handled it the way you handled it, if you did your best, then that should make it easier to release because what else can you give? I think that until we let go of things and stop replaying them, we can't step forward into our next stage.

Being a woman who is moving into her goddess years (which I'm very happy about), I find that a lot of women get stuck wanting to go back to where we used to be. Whatever your age is, "I want to go back to when I wasn't divorced, or when I had a stronger body, or when I made more money," or whatever it is. That's a horrible trap because there's another stage, a literal stage, where there is your "solo in the spotlight" moment. Barbie, take that stage. Your music that you need to dance to now is playing over there. So, you have to let go of the old stuff to get there, and that is challenging for us.

Moneeka: I love that. Thank you so much Leeza for your wisdom and your positivity and for all that you shared with my audience today.

Leeza: And back at you, too.

> *"Show up, do your best, let go of the rest."*
> ~LEEZA GIBBON'S MOM, JEAN

3 KEYS TO USING INTUITION IN REAL ESTATE BY TAPPING INTO YOUR FEMININE STRENGTHS
WITH SASHA BARBER

Moneeka: Sasha Barber is a realtor and broker/owner of Guided Realty, the House of Conscious Real Estate Transactions. She believes that investing in real estate can serve as a vehicle to fund your passions and to best serve your true life purpose. She is on a mission to fulfill your vision for real estate investing and can help you find, negotiate, and oversee a successful real estate transaction in the competitive market in California. She strives to bring conscious business practices to the real estate industry while intuitively guiding you to the best properties that fulfill your investment goals.

For over a decade, Sasha has dedicated her life to personal growth. In the pursuit of personal and professional development, she has become a master Neuro-Linguistic Programming (NLP) practitioner and negotiator. Born and raised in a cold European country, she loves life in Orange County, California and enjoys its sunny, vibrant beach communities with her three young boys and loving, supportive husband.

Whether you are selling, buying, or investing in real estate, allow Sasha to guide you to your next home or investment opportunity easily, effortlessly, worry-free.

I wanted to thank you, Sasha, for coming on this show and sharing your wisdom with my audience.

Sasha: Moneeka, thank you so much for having me. It is such a joy being around you! You always bring my energy up because I like matching your blissfulness!

Moneeka: Anytime! Blissful I am!

Sasha: Yes, you are. By the way, one of my favorite affirmations is: I am bountiful, I am beautiful, I am bliss! I am, I am.

Moneeka: I love that. That is a powerful one!

Sasha: Yes, it is, and so is each woman! Did you know that women are 16 times more powerful and 16 times more intuitive than men? And our inborn capacity to excel in business and in life is 16 times more than of a man? As women, we can accomplish anything if we look deep inside and recognize our divine power!

Moneeka: That's a great reminder! We need to hear it more often because, generationally, a woman has been conditioned to stay small, quiet her voice and opinions, and hide her feelings.

But it has been shifting, fortunately. Today, a woman in many countries around the world is gaining equal rights, is allowed to speak her truth and to be a leader.

Sasha: Yes. And still, even after realizing her purpose, the majority of women unconsciously try to protect themselves by not stepping fully into their power. Those moments are when we need to be there for each other, to remind each other and ourselves to keep unleashing our true potential and our magical powers to create and manifest happiness, success, and prosperity. We are so powerful—we can be the mastermind and the engine. We can conceive, create, and birth a human being, a career, a dream—anything! But we have to have a seed first. We need one thing that comes from outside ourselves to conceive a baby. In our business and life, what we need is a goal to bring forth the manifestation of our dreams and desires. Girl, what's your goal for your life today?

Moneeka: Me? I have quite a few! Keep going!

Sasha: I believe that the keys to success are simple and universal. Simple, but not easy. Today I want us to focus on three keys that can allow you to use your feminine gifts of intuition as a way of conducting your business. Recognize that intuition is innate to us women if we tap into it, trust it, and flow with it. And I hope that as a result, you can make your real estate investing a joyful and rewarding experience, sprinkled with fun and magic.

Moneeka: I can't wait to hear the first key! What is it?

Sasha: It's the most fun one! **Visualize!**

I love the quote, "If you can visualize it, that means it already exists!" The author is unknown because it is a universal truth. And you know it!

In your search for real estate, know exactly what you are looking for. What strategy are you implementing with this purchase? At what price point you are motivated to buy? As you walk through the property in your mind's eye, see the desirable things and eliminate the undesirable ones. Know what you do want and know what you don't want. Make a list.

With that info, you can masterfully and strategically program your search criteria. Some software, like the ones real estate agents use, allow you to add over 200 different parameters. And voila! You either get a short list of properties that is easy to navigate and research further, or you will get zero results. I suggest to use the exact criteria first. If you get no results, begin to step outside the box.

Moneeka: I love that you are talking about this because this is exactly how I search for my properties.

Sasha: It works, doesn't it? I remember working with my friend Irene and her husband Vitali as they were buying their first home for their rapidly growing family. Within the next few months, they would have their third child and a mother-in-law from the Ukraine as their new additions to a tiny one-bedroom rental condo. They needed a home fast as her due date and mother's arrival were fast approaching, but they had a lot of strict criteria, all under a very tight budget! They knew exactly what they wanted and exactly what they didn't want! We kept looking and looking day after day, nothing good was coming up. One day I said desperately: "There are just no homes in good areas of Orange County that can match this strict criteria!" When I said that, it dawned on me! Of course there wasn't—we needed to look outside the box!

So we adjusted the price criteria first and looked at homes whose sellers may be more motivated to sell lower—those with higher DOMs (days on the market). The moment we poked our heads outside the box, their home was there waiting for them! Remember, the moment you can visualize it, it exists! This is what I chose to believe during that experience, and this belief has served me time and time again. After finding that home, we made a lower offer that was still within their budget. Thankfully, the seller was very motivated and we were able to successfully negotiate the gap in price.

Moneeka: What a great story! So, know what you want and visualize it!

Sasha: Exactly! On the technical side, add all of your criteria into the real estate search program you are using or ask your agent to do that for you, and set up auto notifications. That way, when that desirable property hits the market, you know it's time to submit the winning offer! One thing you cannot afford to do in real estate is to procrastinate when you see a deal.

Moneeka: If you see a deal, it's time to negotiate! What is the next key?

Sasha: Key number two: Stay positive.
Your manifesting powers can work like magic. But this magic has a special kind of ingredient: a vibrational frequency of joy, happiness, gratitude, love, peace . . . When you vibrate at this level, everything comes to you easily and effortlessly! I love noticing when I am on fire with positive energy and how much amazingness is happening all around me! Houses get sold quickly, offers get accepted, my clients refer me to their friends and family—all without the daily grind of prospecting, door knocking, boring marketing, etc.

But come on! Let's be honest—does this "on fire" state happen every day? Does it last forever? No! It's a state. It comes and goes. It's easy to say to stay positive when you are in a cave somewhere, where there are no screaming children running around, when there is no need to cook dinner, fold laundry, shop for groceries, run errands, rush the kids to school, dance recitals, soccer practices . . . All while running our careers, trying to get enough sleep, eat healthy foods, drink enough water, maintain healthy relationships, and deal with the ups and downs of our own emotions! It can be overwhelming! And this is non-stop, day after day . . . the story of our lives as women.

And yes, I said that we are 16 times more powerful than men, and yet we are 16 times more emotional than men. And if those emotions are not channeled appropriately through self-care or some kind of uplifting practice like yoga or meditation, or diet and exercise, this can be our downfall. We can become victims of our own insecurities and emotional commotions, creating a great deal of pain and misery for ourselves and others around us. But the biggest issue is: if we allow ourselves to sway into self-pity, guilt, shame, doubt, unworthiness, anger, apathy, self-judgement, we simply stop being magnetic! We stop being magical. Our manifestation powers diminish.

But fear not! It's temporary. Here's the key: when you notice yourself going into that downward emotional spiral, even in the midst of the storm, you must remember there is a sunshine beyond those clouds! The tough time will pass. Just remember that you are a powerful woman who will see it through!

I remember having to remind that to my grandmother. She was depressed from her illness and losing all hope. I flew back to cold, dark Belarus to visit her from sunny California. I remember, as I was nearing my destination and the plane was descending, we got into these thick, heavy November clouds. They stayed above my city, tightly covering it with its grip, not letting through even the tiniest ray of sun. Not one. For months at a time. So my grandmother stopped believing that there was hope, or sun for that matter. If I hadn't just come from up there, from above those clouds, where the sun is so luminous, I wouldn't have believed it either. But I told her: "Hey, the sun is still there, it shines so brightly, just beyond the clouds." I choose to believe that I became her sun then, and together we stayed in that knowing for the few months we had together.

As women we must find the time and the desire to feel good, to have fun, to laugh, and to play! Did you know that playing is a magical form of meditation? It opens your heart and allows your creative spirit to tap into the divine wisdom and alignment! So stop being so serious! Enjoy life!

Moneeka: I can totally bring up so many examples of this. When I am in my bliss, everything does happen magically: deals pop up from nowhere, tenants pay their rent early, money flows effortlessly! And the moment I am off my track, maybe I get into a state of worry, or some fear or insecurity creeps in and I stay there longer than necessary, problems begin to arise. And that is just not so much fun to deal with. But I have trained myself to recognize it and snap out of it!

Sasha: That's wonderful, Moneeka! Because we can be the creator of our own fulfilling destiny and the destroyer of it! And that brings me to the **third key: Trust**.

As a conscious and intuitive woman, you know that you are always guided. If you have a destination, you are definitely guided to it. That's why your goals are so important! If you don't have a particular goal, you are still guided—to your lessons, to your purpose, to your higher self. But the question is: can you trust it?

My best lesson of guidance and trust came to me when I was expecting my third child. I know now that if I didn't follow that guidance presented to me at that time, because of fear, because it seemed weird, because of not knowing how to and the lack of funds, nothing that I have today would exist. Guided Realty wouldn't have come about. I wouldn't be a broker with a huge vision and mission, but perhaps just a mediocre real estate agent. Who I am today would be different. And most importantly for me, I wouldn't be in my power.

Moneeka: So tell me that story! What was that lesson?

Sasha: First, I had to trust the guidance to go to Hawaii to swim with the wild dolphins. It came as a thought one day and wouldn't leave me alone. I was never into dolphins. I knew nothing of the benefits of a prenatal contact with them. I didn't know where to find them. Or why I needed to do that. The thought of HOW was putting me into fear paralysis because I knew it would require my whole family to move to an expensive island for at least a few months, having to leave my husband's graphic designer job, the only thing we could depend on for money at that time. And not to mention, I had already decided I wanted to have another home-water-birth and had to organize that. Thankfully I was already familiar with the process through my second birth, but I knew finding the right midwife and a place for it would require diligent research and some serious cash.

I knew what I was being called to do, but I kept questioning it. Then I started to constantly receive the signs . . . like all the time. For example, as I was driving the kids to school, deep in my thoughts, wondering "Do I really need to do this?" at the next intersection there was a dancing guy on the corner spinning a "Hawaii for 2 - $99" sign. When I thought: "Ok, where do I need to go?" a huge truck "Kona Brewery" crossed the street. When I couldn't fall asleep one night, still pondering upon the same thing, I opened YouTube, and the first video under "Recommended for you" was an oracle card reading for the week that had these three cards: Pregnancy, Affirmation, Do Your Research. To top if off, at the end of the video the host said: "Have a blessed week and Aloha!"

That was it . . . I finally had enough signs and at that moment I decided that I was going to give into this madness and I would give this persistent guidance a try. And as one of the cards suggested, I started my research. And what I saw inspired me so much! I had made a decision: "No matter what I have to do, I am doing this!"

Moneeka: And I suppose you ended up going to Hawaii? Did you find the how?

Sasha: Of course I did! When I made that commitment to my dream, my only real estate client at that time called. He said he wanted to see a house. Then the next day we were in escrow, and in two weeks I was on the plane to Kona, Hawaii, having my dream birth vacation funded!

And it was beyond what I could have imagined; the kind of experience that we got to have, the dolphins we got to swim with, the new friends we made, the gentle natural birth I had, the undisturbed peaceful time with a new baby and the formation of our new family . . . all of these experiences will fill an entire book, one that I am committed to writing, in fact. But that was the reward that I received for following my guidance. But there came another lesson, the one of trust.

When everything comes crumbling down, can YOU trust that it is for the better? In the midst of all the unpleasant changes, can you trust?

Honestly, I was far away from it at first. The situation that we came back to felt so scary and so unfair. From our heavenly trip, we came back home to our dense reality with no leftover funds, with two kids and a newborn baby and straight to:

1. A 60-day notice from our landlord to move out (our rent was low because we had lived there for a very long time).

2. To my husband not getting his job back, or any job, for that matter. He actually got fired the day our baby was born, when he was only gone for four days while still working remotely.

3. To my oldest son getting a denial letter from his school that he was transferring to every year. They were at capacity and weren't accepting transfer students for the new school year.

Welcome back, darlings! The reality missed you!

Trust? How can you tell someone to trust when there is no place to go with small children, no job to pay the bills or to even apply for a new home? Do you think I was able to TRUST in THAT moment? No freaking way! Not only I didn't trust the changes, I tried my best to resist the changes! Isn't it in our nature to do so anyway, to stay small, to fear the unknown? So I wrote convincing letters to the landlord, school, even helped my husband to start a court case because his ex-employer denied his unemployment. So unfair . . .

And there it was, the first glimpse of hope! My first step in the crusade of fixing my life and getting out of the hole was to go to the school district and to get my son assigned to a new school. Easy peasy! The new school's address read 8787 Dolphin Drive! WHAT??? DDDDDolphin dddddddrive? My palms were sweating on the steering wheel when we were first driving up to the school. It was a Dolphin Heaven! There were dolphins everywhere: huge murals on the walls, kids' drawings hanging in rows one better than the other, statues, rugs, school's mascot, t-shirts, jackets, hats. Wow, it felt like the dolphins from Hawaii followed us home, saying: "Don't worry, we got you, we will arrange everything for you! Just trust us and play with us!"

From that day forward, our spirits got high again and we began to trust it. That same week, we found a new home. It was smaller and darker, but tolerable. For years, I have been paying attention to numerology and angels' messages through repeating numbers and the number "111" was one I knew well. It means "Make a wish, the Angels are listening!" Guess what apartment number we had? You guessed it! 111! Living in the apartment #111, I knew I would totally be manifesting my way out quickly!

Shortly thereafter, I received my first ever real estate client referral. Mike and Patty had shopped for a house for three years. All together they wrote sixty-four offers with different agents, with not a single one accepted. Can you even imagine what they had been through? They didn't even believe anymore that their dream of owning a home would ever come true. They had given up hope and took a year off from their house search. When they were ready to do try again, they were magically referred to me.

We spoke on the phone, I ran a search for them, narrowed down the criteria and we got a short list of 11 homes. Out of that list, they choose one home and asked me to show it to them. We arranged a time that weekend, but something told me to look over the list one more time. There was a house in the neighborhood across the street from the one they had chosen. It only had one opportunity for showing, which happened to be during the same timeframe we arranged to meet just five mins away! It was massively underpriced, and they would be accepting offers the next day. But this timeframe coincidence caught my eye and I suggested to Mike and Patty to add that home to our tour.

The home that they had originally selected had a crack right through the foundation, splitting the house in half. It definitely wasn't the one! So we went to the neighborhood across the street to the other house, barely catching the last few minutes of their one and only open house.

Coming up to the home, Patty saw the porch swing that was in her visualization. Mike saw tall evergreen trees that protected the home and gave it privacy, key point that was important to him. And this was it! They knew it the moment they saw it that they were home! We met with the owners and their agent and chatted briefly as they gave us the tour of their prized possession, their beloved home that they had to leave due to relocation.

I remember standing outside this house, holding my three-month-old baby Maika on my hip (I was breastfeeding and had to take him everywhere I went, including client appointments). We were about to discuss offer details when, for the first time, I had a moment to pause and notice Mike's hat. With big white letters it said DOLPHINS! Surprised, I asked: "Why does your hat say 'dolphins'?" I looked over at my "dolphin baby," as we lovingly called him, and Mike replied: "I have been supporting this charity that protects dolphins around the world by donating money for twenty-five years! This hat was the gift they sent me!"

Moneeka: Can I guess? They got the house, right?

Sasha: Of course they did! That was a gift from the dolphins to Mike and Patty for taking care of them! But remember, this house was massively underpriced, which was the strategy the seller chose to use to get as many people through the doors as possible in one short window. So, there was a bidding war with 10 other offers on the table. I suggested that we submit a fair market value, and even though there was another buyer offering even more money, for the house, the seller still chose Mike and Patty's offer! He said, "I don't know what is it about you guys, but I really want you to live here!"

Moneeka: Was that how Guided Realty was born?

Sasha: Yes. I remember coming home that day, feeling so magically supported and guided. I looked back at everything that had happened that day, and I realized that we were all GUIDED! First, my clients were GUIDED to me (there is more to the story there, but that's an interview for another day). Then, I noticed and recognized the sign of a peculiar time frame for this open house that they weren't even interested in because it didn't look like anything special from the pictures. And they didn't want to participate in yet another bidding war as they were sick and tired of that "game" in the last three years of house hunting. My sister-in-law was guided to come unannounced from far away to visit my kids' soccer games that morning; that allowed me to leave early to go meet my clients and to make that open house. Mike and Patty weren't supposed to come early, either, due to their passport appointment, but magically it finished quickly. So many things had to arrange themselves in order for us to even make it to this house on time on that Saturday, and for their offer to get accepted on the first try on the home of their dreams!

That night, the name and the ideas behind Guided Realty were born with all of its values and guiding principles. And from that day forward, it never ceases to amaze me how guided we truly are if we train ourselves to notice the signs.

Moneeka: It's so true! Can you trust your guidance? Have you been shown the signs, but chose to ignore them? Or have you followed the signs? Where did they lead you? Can you trust it, when the outer circumstances look like nothing is working out? Do you have enough patience to say: "This was not meant for me because something better is around the corner?" Can you believe that when things aren't happening the way you want them to or in a time frame you want them to happen, it is because they aren't meant to happen, or it is just not for your highest and best good?

Sasha: I can recall quite a few times when my clients had said with a sigh of relief: "Thank God that other offer didn't go through because if it did, I wouldn't have gotten this better house!" Or, "I wish I didn't have to worry about being rejected by just knowing that a better investment was waiting for me with better terms and lower interest rates!"

Moneeka: Now I can totally understand what it means when you talk about trust!

Sasha: And also, I believe that when you are aligned with your goal, with a clear vision, and a compelling dream, things will happen the right way, right away! You won't have to waste time making offers on homes that are not the best option for you.

Moneeka: That takes some work on yourself. Even in my "Blissful Real Estate Investing Workshop," I teach about how to remove obstacles that may be sabotaging your success.

Sasha: I am so glad that you do! Because if you want to be successful in this business and in life, working on yourself is a necessity. One of the best self-development trainings I took was the one where I met you, Moneeka! It was an advanced NLP training which taught us to recognize limiting beliefs, negative emotions, and values conflicts, and to break through them in all aspects of life. Our trained eye for negative patterns is very handy when working with our clients, isn't it? Why wouldn't you want to resolve whatever may be blocking your success? It is the only way to stop doing the same thing over and over again expecting a different result!

Moneeka: Exactly! Another thing that I teach in my workshops is about finding the right agent for you because your agent is like gold. They are the person that is going to make or break your business. They can show you things you didn't even know existed. One of the big things to keep in mind when you are looking for an agent is to make sure that your agent is on board with your strategy. Some agents don't want their clients to buy certain properties because in the agent's eyes it will not be a good investment. Sometimes an agent may impose their opinions or they won't work as hard to get you that property that you want as an investor. It is very important to make sure you get somebody like Sasha who is willing to create success for her client. And that is key.

I have been working with an agent in the San Francisco Bay Area for over 15 years, and he was totally on board with whatever harebrained idea I come up with. I started buying houses in areas that were going to appreciate, like my primary residences. We turned those into rentals one at a time as I moved. Then I started buying rentals at a really cheap price. Now I am in construction. But as I moved and changed my strategy, he had to be able to move with me. He had to be flexible and to trust me that I knew what I was doing, all the while offering his expertise to achieve the goals that I was and am trying to reach. He was invaluable. I was in Thailand, and he actually texted me and said, "I have a property that matches your parameters. I think it would be really good. Do you want me to make an offer on it?" and he sent me pictures. I trusted him because I had been working with him for 12 years. He made an offer that was accepted, and then when I flew home from vacation, I took a look at it. The timeframe, I think, was three days because I could still back out of an offer then. I looked at the property and I went with the purchase. But that level of trust can't happen if you keep jumping to new agents or you have an agent who doesn't understand what you are about and what you are trying to accomplish.

Sasha: Yes, absolutely! I am the type of agent who will work with you to align your strategy with your vision of success, and I will hold you accountable to it!

Moneeka: Sasha, this has been so much fun, but we are coming to the end of our time together. Could you tell my readers how they can get in touch with you?

Sasha: Yes. You can email me directly at sasha@guidedrealty.com. I also wanted to give our readers a gift. Is that okay?

Moneeka: Yes!

Sasha: If you do business or look for real estate in the state of California, I would like to offer you a hot list of homes in your market place that is based on your criteria and your strategies. This is a free service and there is no obligation. I am happy to do this for you because I know how overwhelming this can be to get started with the buying process. And where do you start? You start with research, you look at listings, you go visit those properties, and you calculate different scenarios. That is how you move one foot in front of the other to your success.

One of my passions is serving women through their pregnancy and childbirth as a doula. I can prepare a woman on all levels to have the birth that she desires, and I am with her throughout the birth itself. I am there in person being her support physically, mentally, emotionally during every moment of the intense experience, constantly reminding her and connecting her back to her innate wisdom, her body, and her baby.

In your real estate investing journey, I can do the same for you, being there through the birthing of your real estate dreams. As you birth one deal at a time, one flip at a time, I am here as someone you can consult with, gain professional opinion, talk through your "what ifs," fears, concerns, risks, and rewards. I am here, so you can double your intuitive powers and run your business with ease and grace!

We may be bound by the geographical location of your business, but I have been building a national referral network of real estate agents and brokers who share similar beliefs and values. So feel free to reach out! For now, Guided Realty is spreading its conscious business practices throughout California with its base in Southern California. When clients choose to work with me, whether they are in San Francisco or San Diego, I will travel for them—if I know that I can serve. My experience has proven that with clients who are open to my process, and with some prep work, we can get things done quickly. And this is my gift!

Moneeka: You are so gifted, Sasha! What is one daily practice that contributes to your success?

Sasha: I have been a practitioner and a teacher of Kundalini yoga. This practice gives me so much awareness. It was a catapult to developing my intuition and to living my life and running my business on a more conscious level. As a daily practice I choose one of the meditations and stay with it for some time. I would like to teach you one of my favorites. It is an easy and short but powerful meditation for women, called the "Grace of God." When you practice this meditation, it can help yo u to develop mental clarity, effective communication, patience, strength and radiance, which can allow you to go through the challenges of life and business with grace. Just send a request email to iAmTheGraceOfGod111@gmail.com, and the instructional video will be sent to you automatically.

Moneeka: Thank you!

> *"A woman in harmony with her spirit is like a river flowing. She goes where she will without pretense and arrives at her destination prepared to be herself and only herself."*
> ~MAYA ANGELOU

CREATE FREEDOM OF TIME AND SPACE
WITH JACQUELINE T. HUYNH

Moneeka: Today I'd like to welcome to the show our guest, Jacqueline T.D. Huynh!

Born in Saigon, Vietnam and raised in Orange County, California, Jacqueline is the firstborn of five girls. In 1975, at 8 years old, she and her family escaped imminent death from the Vietnam War. They arrived in the United States as refugees with only the clothes on their backs, the hope of the American dream, and the commitment to succeed to honor the family who were left behind or perished.

Jacqueline is a keynote speaker, bestselling author, and coach on 3 major topics: Generational Wealth, Family Legacy, and Leadership. She helps families create cash-flow through real estate investing, become financially free, and leave a profound memorable legacy to their loved ones.

Her book, Your Amazing Itty Bitty Book on Family Leadership: 15 Simple Tips Successful Companies Use That Families Can Implement At Home is an Amazon #1 Bestseller and her second book, True Legacy Wealth: Creating Generational Wealth Through Real Estate Investing, was published in March 2019.

She is also the host and producer of a weekly parenting podcast called Parent Pump Radio.

Moneeka: Hey there, Jacqueline, how are you? Welcome to the show!

Jacqueline: It is a pleasure and an honor to be on your show. I listen to your podcast. It's wonderful.

Moneeka: I'm glad you enjoy listening. Now before we get into this hot topic about how you define wealth, tell us why you're so passionate about wealth and legacy.

Jacqueline: Well, Moneeka, sometimes it takes something tragic to happen in your life for you to wake up and see it in a whole new perspective. That's what happened to me. On July 15, 2019, at 8:41 a.m., I received a text from one of my sisters saying, "Paramedics taking Dad to ER now." At 9:39 a.m., I received another message saying, "Everybody needs to come now. Daddy had a brain bleed. The doctor said he won't survive this." And at 11:35 p.m., my dad's heart stopped beating. My dad suffered from a massive brain hemorrhage that filled the right side of his brain by the time he got to the hospital.

Moneeka: I'm so sorry to hear that, Jacqueline. My heart goes out to you and your family.

Jacqueline: Thank you, Moneeka. My dad was only 76 years old. He thought he had more time. We thought he had more time. He was a quiet man who never spoke ill of anyone. We knew him as a strong man who served his family and his country, Vietnam and the United States, with pride. It was his mission that we ALWAYS knew our family roots and Vietnam's history and consistently be in service. In the weeks that followed, I found a short 20-page memoir that he had typed up about his life. In it he spoke about his struggles: Of his parent's separation when he was around 10, his plight to escape Vietnam to get to us, and the conflict he endured trying to raise a family in a completely unfamiliar country. We come from a culture where men are supposed to be stoic to show their strength, but reading about his fears, adversities, and inner conflicts actually made me feel incredibly closer to him and appreciate him more than I ever have. He became more human to me and someone I could relate to.

Moneeka: Wow, that's incredible.

Jacqueline: That's why it's so important to me to start the movement of breaking down the misperception that vulnerability is weak and wealth is just about money.

Moneeka: You're right. The more we allow ourselves to show that we struggle and have low points, the more relatable we are and the walls start coming down.

Jacqueline: Yes, so sit down with your loved ones. Talk about your life. Talk about the downs as well as the ups. Talk about your fears, your struggles, when you were sad, and so on. This is how your legacy will continue. This is part of your multi-generational wealth.

Moneeka: That is beautiful, Jacqueline. Let's get right into this hot topic. Let's define wealth from your perspective.

Jacqueline: This is the 2nd misconception because people think wealth is money or financial assets. However, money or financial wealth is actually a symptom or byproduct of who you know and what you know.

Moneeka: Oh, I love that!

Jacqueline: Freedom of time and space, which is the ability to do what you want, when you want, with whomever you want, and for as long as you want. That's how I measure true wealth.

Moneeka: Although I have never defined it that way, I would absolutely agree with that.

Jacqueline: There are three parts to wealth, and I think you will agree with this. The first one is who you know. These are the human assets: your family, your friends, your clients, your business associates, your connections, and even your values, your beliefs, and your health.

The second part of wealth is your intellectual assets, which is what you know and includes your education, your skills, your knowledge, and your experience.

The third part is your financial assets. This is just a symptom of what you know and who you know. If someone has the human and intellectual assets and they lose all their financial assets, you can put them anywhere in the world and because of who they know and what they know, they will come back.

Moneeka: It is so interesting that you are qualifying wealth in that way, because I know many real estate coaches who are out there talking about the numbers, the strategy, and the property. But the thing that they miss is the human element. I've been bringing this more into the market; because here is the truth: the numbers can do whatever they do, the market can do whatever it does, but you make your business. People do business with people. They don't do business with houses or numbers. People do business with people. And it is important to really get that real estate is a people business. Thank you for emphasizing that.

Jacqueline: Absolutely! We hear the statement "He has a wealth of knowledge." That's associating knowledge with wealth. Of course, money is certainly a part of wealth, but it's a symptom of who you know and what you know.

Moneeka: Awesome! Tell us about the four ways to make money.

Jacqueline: Regardless of what your business is, there are four ways to make money: Cash flow, leverage, appreciation, and rules.

Moneeka: Let's break each one down because there is so much I want to talk about in each of these areas!

Jacqueline: Cash flow is when money is coming in. How are you making money? With a J-O-B, you are trading time for money, and you don't get any more money than that. If you have a job, you are limited in your income because you will never make more money than the person above you. When you own a business, you have unlimited potential in cash flow, and you are not necessarily exchanging money for time. This is why we urge people to get into a business. Real estate investing is an easy way to start a business and passively earn money while you have a job. With a business in real estate, you can make money while you are sleeping!

Moneeka: Right! There are several different kinds of cash flow. One is the "more money now." Whether it is from your work or from your business, this is money that pays the bills. The second is "more money later." This is everything you have in your pipeline that you are working towards. When you are in a job, the "more money later" is what you invest in your work to get a promotion. When you are in the business of real estate, these are the tenants that you hope to be working with later. This is when you buy a property that is cutting even now and you hope to cash flow later. The third is cash flow for the "business of running life." This is everything that you save for later, and we talked about this in appreciation. You are earning money for big life

events, like a child's college education, a child's wedding, your own retirement, a big trip. Cash flow shows up in a lot of different buckets.

Jacqueline: We probably can spend 30 minutes on each of the four ways!

Moneeka: Yes, we could, but we only have time to share little bits on each one now.

Jacqueline: The second way to make money is leverage. This is when you are leveraging what you have to create more money. For example, in a business, you can hire employees, borrow money against the business for a loan, or hire a marketing consultant. You can use the money to make more money for yourself. This doesn't really work in a job.

Moneeka: Right! In real estate, leverage is the magic secret of making money. Let's say, for instance, you get a loan to buy a $100,000 home. That is a $100,000 asset. The bank takes 80% of the responsibility for that asset, but you are only taking a 20% risk, which is the 20% down payment you paid. Now, you have control of a $100,000 asset for only $20,000. There is no other place where you can get that kind of wealth.

Jacqueline: If you use leverage.

Moneeka: Right! What's really exciting is when the property value goes up. To keep the numbers simple, let's say your property doubles in value in 10 years, so it's now worth $200,000. How much have you made? Have you doubled your money? No! You have increased your money by 5 times from your original investment; you have gone from a value of $100,000 to $200,000 but you only put 20% down. You put down $20,000 that has now gone up by $100,000! Now, if you don't pay your mortgage the bank will take away your house. But just think about this: banks are giving you the opportunity to live in a beautiful place that you own. The bank will take 80% of the risk so you can take advantage of your home's appreciation. That is true leverage towards wealth.

Jacqueline: And here is the other thing about leverage. Once you have properties, you won't need to take money out of your own pocket to make a down payment. You can use your properties as collateral and get an equity loan to invest in more properties. The more properties you have, the less money you have to take out of your own pocket.

Moneeka: That's right! The leverage increases as you own more properties. This is why real estate is exciting, and you can't do this anywhere else. It's amazing.

Jacqueline: Yes! The third way to make money is through appreciation. If you own a home you easily understand this concept. Things go up in value. Real estate historically goes up. That is the one thing we know, that over time—if you hang on to real estate—the value will go up. That is another way you make money while you were sleeping. You can sell it, you can leverage it and borrow more money, and you can leave it to your kids. It is something tangible that can be passed down through multiple generations.

A job on the other hand, doesn't appreciate in value. It doesn't go up. You can't sell it, you can't leave it to your kids, and you can't share the people and colleagues that you have met with anybody else. It just stays with you.

Moneeka: Appreciation is my favorite strategy.

Jacqueline: The fourth way to make money is with Rules. While some people have received some surprise tax bills after filing their returns, businesses, on the other hand, continue to avoid paying taxes—thanks to tax credits, loopholes, and exemptions. Amazon paid $0 in taxes on $11,200,000,000 in profit for 2018 and they didn't pay any taxes in 2017.

If you are going to play the game, then you need to know the rules to take full advantage of the game. Real estate investing can be an exciting and fun game. You'll need to be knowledgeable about the laws of owning a business, taxation rules, loopholes, and exemptions. All the tax rules and laws are set up for businesses to take advantage of.

There are many ways that business owners and real estate investors can take advantage of all the rules. For example, you can hire and pay your kids to work for you in your business, helping you manage your real estate—you are teaching them how to do it—and you can write it off as a tax deduction. Your children can now use this money to pay for college. You are paying for their education with pre-tax money. But if you have a job, you have to make the money, pay taxes on it, and then you pay for their education. (Check with your tax consultant on all the rules and specifics on this.)

Moneeka: There are many nuances around that. If you start paying them at age 12 or 15, they can begin to save more at an earlier age. There are many other nuances that a tax consultant is going to be able to help you with.

Jacqueline: Yes. Now, if you have a job, then the benefit that comes from Rules don't really apply to you. In my second book, my co-author is a tax, business, and real estate attorney. He will tell you that the available deductions in the IRS code book for W-2 employees is very thin. However, the majority of the book contains all the credits, loopholes, and exemptions for businesses. One of the biggest benefits of owning a business when you know the rules is you get to decide if, when, and how much you are going to pay in taxes.

Moneeka: I want to add here that this a lot of information and it feels overwhelming. This is why we go back to the idea that real estate is a people business. You hire the pros to advise you on all of this.

Jacqueline: Absolutely!

Moneeka: The pros will tell you everything you need to do; they will help minimize the work, which will minimize your stress and increase your money. In the United States, the government has set these rules in place to help us to thrive, even if we don't believe that. People complain about high taxes. But taxes pay for the way we get to live in this country. The government really wants people to feel committed to living here and to their communities, so there are rules and benefits for those of us who own real estate that allow you to grow your wealth faster. Even though some of the rules feel intimidating, understand that they are there for your benefit and you can take advantage of those benefits. We have many international listeners, and I don't know about tax rules in other countries so be sure to talk to a local expert!

Jacqueline: You made a good point. You don't have to know all these things. In Napoleon Hill's book, Think and Grow Rich, Hill recounts Henry Ford's statement that he is one touch away from any expert that he needs, and they help him. You don't have to be an expert on the rules, or business strategies, or even any of the things required to maintain a house. Instead the most important thing you can do is create a team. A team of people you trust and who are experts in what they do.

Moneeka: Nice! Thank you for that.

Jacqueline: You're welcome.

Moneeka: Let's do a little bit more of a comparison of a J-O-B versus a business.

Jacqueline: We already talked about the four ways to make money. When I think about the potential of making money in a job, it is very limited compared to a business or investing in real estate. It is important to re-member that real estate investing is a business. You can't look at yourself as being a landlord. You are a business owner. You run a real estate business.

When you compare a business with a job, all the skills that you have learned, all the training, and all the connections that you have made no longer exist when you retire or when you pass away; that's the end of it. It is not something that is multi-generational, you can't leave it to an heir, you can't give it to somebody. You can't even sell your job. It is only worth what you have put into it.

I come from an Asian family, and everything is about the family. Think about a local Asian restaurant you eat at. You will probably see the mom, the grandmother, and the kids working there. This concept is really important. This is a family business, so your training, your skills, your knowledge, and all the connections that you have made are passed on to your kids. They know everything you know, so when you retire, or pass away, it transfers automatically. This is the legacy they inherit from you. Another great thing about having a real estate business is that it will go up in value; your job will not.

Moneeka: I love that you say that real estate is a business. I think people detach real estate so it is just an investment. It is its own entity. But there is a very different mindset when you talk about something being a business, rather than something being an investment. An investment is something that happens outside of you and the market controls it. A business is something that you make choices about, you manage, and that benefits you directly on a day-to-day basis.

Jacqueline: Right! And in a business, you are constantly learning and growing with your assets. When you think of yourself as a landlord, you detach yourself. You don't involve your kids. You don't involve your family. You pay the bills, you take the late night calls, you do the repairs by yourself, and you go over all the paperwork by yourself. However, if you think of yourself as a business owner, you can get your children involved by teaching them how to work the business instead.

I used to be an estate planning paralegal, and the co-author of my second book is an estate planning attorney. We remember countless times when adult children would come in after their parents passed away. The children are left with a portfolio of real estate holdings that they fight over or they sell it and spend the proceeds on bills, cars, or vacations; then it's gone. Their parents never taught them what to do with the real estate. For the children, it was just money to fight over and enjoy. On the contrary, if they had learned from their parents how to invest, they could have had a paycheck for the rest of their lives and their children's lives. That is what real estate investing can do, it can give cash flow security to future generations.

Moneeka: Great advice, Jacqueline! Next, could you tell us the three mistakes people make toward their financial freedom?

Jacqueline: Yes. **The first mistake is not taking advantage of being in a business.** From our earlier discussion, I hope it is very clear why you would want some kind of business. A business is the same whether you are a landlord or selling flowers or coaching. You want to be in a business so you can take advantage of all the four ways to make money and acquire real wealth: human and intellectual assets that generate financial assets, which you can pass down to future generations. People may think that they can't have a business because they work nine to five or because they are a teacher or a firefighter. That is the beauty about real estate investing and my unique turnkey real estate investing program: you don't have to quit your job. We find, analyze, rehab, and manage the properties for you. You purchase and prosper. If you love your 9-5 job, then keep it AND have a business so you can take advantage of the tax benefits. And when you do retire—which you will—you will have learned how to run a business, which you then can step right into.

Moneeka: Nice!

Jacqueline: **The second mistake is not planning for multi-generational wealth.** As parents, we want to take care of our kids, but many people don't know how to do that except for in the moment. For people who are wealthy—like the Carnegies or the Vanderbilts—their future generations will be taken care of because each generation is taught how to accumulate and pass their wealth on. I think it is a shame that we spend all our life meeting people, connecting with them, establishing all these lifelong relationships, acquiring knowledge and skills, and then it all dies with us. When you have a business, all your relationships can be passed down in the business and it can flow easily to the next generation.

Moneeka: I love that! I don't believe it is anyone's intention to just live day to day and not plan for the future. Much of the time, it is because we don't know how or don't know where to go.

Jacqueline: People don't have the time and/or knowledge on how to enter real estate investing. They hear scary stories about tenants who trash the properties and the owners are stuck with the cost of fixing the mess, or investment property that was bought in the wrong place and when the market crashed the owner lost all their money. In our program, we have experts in place, so your chances of experiencing these scary stories are drastically reduced. We saw what people are afraid of, what was so hard as an entry point, and we have eliminated that. This way a teacher, a firefighter, or a postal worker can take advantage of investing in real estate with very little knowledge and know that our team is here to teach and help them.

Moneeka: What I really love is that you focus on moms who are trying to plan for their children.

Jacqueline: Absolutely! Moms are the silent leader of their family. We are like the board of directors. We let the dad be the CEO. I heard a joke that says, "I let my husband make all the important decisions but I decide which decisions are important."

When it comes to planning for the future, I find that moms see farther ahead in the future. The dads are working and make money for the household and planning for today. The other great thing about most moms is that they are great with emotional intelligence and intuition. Statistically, over 80% of self-help books are bought by women, which is a testament that we are always wanting to learn and grow.

Moneeka: Absolutely.

Jacqueline: Your show is great because it focuses on women. There are more women's movements today because we want to be independent, even if we have a husband. I have married clients who are set because their husband makes money, but they still want to create their own financial freedom. These women want to have their own portfolio, they want to be financially literate, and they want to understand business. They don't want to depend on their husband. The great thing about now is that we are not in our husband's shadow like it was in the 1950s and 1960s; we can be our own powerful women.

Moneeka: Yes, your marriage is a partnership! In my household, my husband makes the income for our lifestyle, and I manage the plan for our future. He plans for today and I plan for tomorrow. I will be the person that retires us, but he is paying for all the fun that we have, our lifestyle, our travel. And we always live within whatever he is making. He creates the budget, the parameters for the budget, and then I am creating for the future. Women should definitely be involved, even if they are all set up because their husband makes a lot of money—yay you! So you go and do the future planning. And when the time to retire comes, both of you will be happy that you paid attention to the future because your husband was out there, busting his butt, working hard to give you your lifestyle.

Jacqueline: Yes! And remember that you are going to be an empty-nest-er one day. If you start a business and grow it, you'll have your own passion and purpose outside of being a mom. You will not all of a sudden be alone with nothing to do when the kids leave. You will have built this business and included your kids.

Moneeka: Wow!

Jacqueline: Teach your kids, involve them in your business, and they will thrive. And when they thrive, you thrive, and the whole family thrives. Our youngest client is 14 now, and she bought her first property when she was 11. Now the property is in a trust in her parents' name, but it was from money she received and earned! Her parents took her to meet the vendors to learn what they do and to see the properties. She is now learning how to run her own investment business.

Moneeka: Isn't that amazing?

Jacqueline: Yes!

> **Buying real estate is not just for adults, not just for dads or for moms; it is for the whole family!**

This is important for the listeners to understand.

Moneeka: This is such great information.

Jacqueline: And there is still the #1 mistake people make.

Moneeka: Oh! Tell me!

Jacqueline: Okay! **The third mistake people make is overlooking passive income opportunities.** Warren Buffett said, "**If you don't find** a **way to make money while you sleep, you will work until you die.**" You and I understand this very well because real estate is a great way to make that money while you sleep. You have rental income coming in, your property is appreciating, and you can leverage it and earn money back by applying the rules. You will also have people working and making money for you. This could be your assistant or property manager or plumber or other professionals on your team who are helping you.

You are not a landlord. You are a business owner who takes advantage of all the rules, credits, loopholes, and exemptions so you can pass your wealth on to your heirs.

For our listeners, do you have a job you can't or don't want to quit? Then real estate investing is a good place to start because it can help you lower your taxes—along with all the other advantages we spoke about.

Moneeka: Right! Real estate investors have a different perspective on passive income than most people do. I always buy high-end properties. When I purchase a house, I am looking for appreciation, and I usually have to wait for my passive income. But by the time I am getting the passive income, I have trained my tenants and my team so well that it really is passive. It is really about the systems you create to make the passive income happen. You do actually make money while you sleep. It is not just something you are giving lip service to, which many people do. Systems and your team are really important to creating that passive income.

Jacqueline: Absolutely! Systems will help you propel that passive income higher and higher. So the number one mistake that people make is overlooking passive income opportunities. Those are the three super tips to help your audience get started. And don't forget about sharing your vulnerabilities and stories as part of your intellectual assets. It is a key factor in building the connection with your loved ones to create true generational wealth and legacy.

Moneeka: Wow! That was such good information. Jacqueline, I know you have a special gift for our audience. Could you share that with us now?

Jacqueline: Okay! I am offering a 45-minute strategy session. You tell me where you are now, where you want to be, and what are some of the obstacles in your way. We will look at that together to see how we can implement a strategy of passive income by making you a business owner so that you can go to sleep at night, make money, and sleep peacefully knowing that you and your family are set. They can call me at (424) 262-4433 or book a time to speak with me on my website at www.IntegrativeLegacy.com. Go to the Contact Us tab.

Moneeka: I want the audience to know that your special gift is really generous. Not everybody who comes on the show wants to give out their phone number, and that is reasonable, because we have thousands of listeners.

Jacqueline: Yes!

Moneeka: But when someone does give out their phone number, you can see that they are really interested in making sure that you get the personal attention that you need to get started. Take advantage of this; Jacqueline is offering to do something beautiful for you and this is an opportunity we don't always get. Jacqueline, thank you very much for that. You would normally charge $400 for that session?

Jacqueline: Yes! This is a private session with me. Not with an associate. I will also utilize my team of experts to help answer any questions that I may not be able to answer.

Moneeka: Nice! When you call Jacqueline, mention my name, because she is giving a longer session to my listeners.

Jacqueline: Yes! Moneeka is very special and dear to my heart, and if you are listening to Moneeka, you are definitely on my special list, also.

Moneeka: Okay! Are you ready Jacqueline, for our three rapid-fire questions?

Jacqueline: Let's go!

Moneeka: Jacqueline, tell us one super tip on getting started in real estate investing.
Jacqueline: An important strategy, which was helpful for me, is to set aside a certain amount of money you make to pay yourself first. Start building the fund you need to start a real estate business. If I were in my 30s or 40s, I would not put it into a retirement account right now. I would put it aside and start investing in real estate, because that IS your retirement. Take whatever you can afford and put it into a separate account to start building up to invest in real estate. Then contact me so I can help you get started right.

Moneeka: Okay! Second question, what is one strategy for being successful in real estate investing?

Jacqueline: Build a team you can trust and who are experts in their field. This way you don't have to know everything. They will help you analyze the right area, buy the right property, manage it, create cash flow, and be able to mitigate most of what could go wrong. Our team is here to help our clients with everything they need to know about real estate investing. We love to share our knowledge and help you create financial freedom. It's more fun to party with others than alone.

Moneeka: Perfect! The last question, Jacqueline: what would you say is one daily practice that contributes to your success?

Jacqueline: Copy success. Success is a formula, and instead of trying to create your own, look at how other people have been successful and copy them. A few regular practices that I do are meditate to increase my intuition and read a book or listen to a podcast. I want to learn from those who are successful, such as Warren Buffett, Robert Kiyosaki, Richard Branson, Tony Robbins, or Oprah. I learn about their businesses, their daily practices, their mindset, their thoughts, and their beliefs. I follow these people and visit their Facebook pages to see what they are saying. I also have my own coaches and mentors that I check in with. Did you know that 75% of CEOs in Fortune 500 companies have a coach or a mentor?

Moneeka: Yes, they do! And I was one of those coaches for a long time.

Jacqueline: There you go. These people are the top of the food chain, and yet they are looking at someone to coach them. You will find that successful people, successful athletes, successful entertainers from Oprah to Michael Jordan to Beyoncé have coaches.

Moneeka: Coaches and mentors can give you a different perspective. Because all you have the capacity to do is act on what you know and understand, so having a different perspective can completely open up other possibilities for you.

Jacqueline: I don't know what I would have done without all my coaches throughout the years; I don't know what I would do without all the successful people I admire. So, the answer to your question is always look for someone who knows more than you. Copy success.

Moneeka: I love that. This has been such a fun, informative conversation. Thank you so much, Jacqueline.

Jacqueline: You are welcome!

Moneeka: All of this sharing has been wonderful.

Jacqueline: It's so fun helping people. What you and I do is all about helping. I love it when I can make someone feel better, do better, be better. Then I feel like I have left a mark on this world. And that was my purpose, I left some sort of legacy.

Moneeka: Thank you for that generosity, Jacqueline.

Jacqueline: You are welcome.

"Legacy is not leaving something FOR people.
It's leaving something IN people."
~PETER STROPLE

Finding Investment Capital Blissfully

In order to decide on a strategy to build wealth, first you need to know how much capital you have access to. Here are some ways to find the capital you need blissfully.

HOW TO GET ALL THE MONEY
YOU NEED TO BUY REAL ESTATE
WITH JAY CONNER

Moneeka: Today, I am so excited to welcome back to the show Jay Conner. Jay has been buying and selling houses for 14 years in a population of only 40,000 people, with profits averaging $64,000 per transaction. That's a lot. He's rehabbed over 300 houses and been involved in over $52 million in transactions. For the past seven years, Jay has completely automated his seven-figure income business to where he works in his business less than 10 hours a week. Now that's my definition of bliss!

Jay has consulted one-on-one with over 2000 real estate investors and has managed to raise $2.15 million in less than 90 days in private money when he was cut off from the banks. He's a national speaker on the topics of private money, automation, and foreclosures. He's the bestselling author of The New Masters of Real Estate: Getting Deals Done in the New Economy. And Jay is a leading expert on private lending, marketing, and business development. He lives with his beautiful wife Carol Joy in North Carolina.

Welcome to the show, Jay!

Jay: Well, hello Moneeka! And it's so great to see you here on the show.

Moneeka: Yeah, you and I hate real estate, don't we?

Jay: I mean, when exciting things are going on in your life, it's hard not to talk about them.

Moneeka: That's right. And how many people really get it? That's why community is so important. That's why having people, mentors, community, and friends who are in real estate and doing it is so important. Because then, you can share your excitement and they're not going to pull you down. They're not going to say, "Oh, the market's going down." They're not going to put all of their fear into you. Instead they will help to build you up. Wouldn't you agree?

Jay: Absolutely. I was just reading one of the famous quotes again this morning when I was doing my morning reading. And that is, "You can pretty much tell what someone's future is looking like by the books they read and the people they hang around." So, to your viewers and listeners, be careful who you're hanging around because if you're hanging around the naysayers, it's not going to build you up, it's only going to pull you down.

Moneeka: That's right. It slows you down. I'm always excited to talk to you for the same reasons. Let's dive in. Let's talk about private money, which is my favorite topic to talk to you about.

Jay: Excellent. I'm ready.

Moneeka: Awesome. First of all, let's define private money, and what's the difference between private money and hard money?

Jay: Okay. So, private money is simply when we're doing business with individuals to fund our investments. We're not doing business with institutions, we're not doing business with banks, we're not doing business with companies—we're doing business with individuals. So, a private lender is simply an individual just like you, just like me, that loans money from their investment capital or (and this is really important) they loan money from their retirement accounts to us real estate investors to get higher rates and a return that are safe and secure.

So, the reason I say that's so important about retirement accounts is this. My wife, Carol Joy, and I now have 48 different individuals, private lenders, who are loaning money to us to fund our deals. And over half of them, Moneeka, are using their retirement funds to fund our deals. And so, that's why it's so important . . . and we may not have time to talk too much about this on this show. So, maybe in one of our deep-dive conversations later, we can talk about how crucial it is for us as real estate investors to establish a relationship with a self-directed IRA company. And the reason for that is if I didn't have that in place, I would not have over half of my funding with my private lenders.

Moneeka: And also, if you set it up for yourself, you're setting yourself up for an amazing retirement that most people can't even imagine.

Jay: Oh, that's true.

Moneeka: So it goes both ways.

Jay: Absolutely. With self-directed IRAs, when you have one yourself, you can be a private lender yourself. I'm a real estate investor. I use my retirement funds in a self-directed IRA to loan out to real estate investors. So, that's a neat way to make passive income. But here's what's so cool about those self-directed IRAs. The income potential per year is unlimited, penalty-free, and tax-free. So, people can use their retirement funds to loan out and be a private lender to real estate investors, or they can actually use their retirement funds to invest on their own once they are in a self-directed IRA or a Third Party Custodian, as the IRS calls it.

Moneeka: Yeah. This is something to think about. We are limited on how much money we can contribute to our IRAs each year. But what Jay just said is, and this is true, we're not limited on how much we can make in those IRAs.

So Jay, thank you. Now, let's just talk a little bit about what the advantages are of private money as opposed to other kinds of funding.

Jay: Sure. So, let me first compare private money to hard money. Moneeka, I'm sure you've got a lot of viewers and listeners out there that may have borrowed hard money or they've heard about hard money. Private money is not hard money. Most of the time when we say hard money, we're talking about a broker. Most of the time hard money funding is a broker of money, a company that has gone out and raised private capital from individuals that then marks up the interest rate, charges fees, points, and origination fees, etc., and then charges a higher interest rate to the real estate investor.

For example, with private money versus hard money, the average interest rate as of your show today, is 14% nationwide for hard money loans. From this world of private money doing business with individuals, it's just 8%. Hard money lenders charge points. The average points they charge are four points or origination fees. There's no origination fees with private lenders. Hard money lenders charge extension fees if you haven't cashed out by the time the term expires. The average extension fee right now is two points. We're up to 20% in the first year in hard money, but we're still at 8% with private lenders.

Another big difference, Moneeka, is that when it comes to hard money, most of the time they're only going to advance 60 to 85% of our purchase price, regardless of how good the deal is. Of course, we have to come up with the other balance of the purchase. In this world of private money, we get 100% of our purchase price. And then if we are rehabbing the house, we'll get 100% of our rehab money up front. So, the world of private money just puts us so much more in control of our business.

And there's no credit check. In the world of private money, your credit's got nothing to do with how much private money you can get. Hard money lenders are going to pull your credit. So, as you mentioned before, in my live events, we dive deep into this as far as differentiating the difference between hard money and private money. But those are some of the most important differences between hard money and private money.

Moneeka: That's a lot. Tell me your favorite reason for using private money. Just highlight one.

Jay: If I had to boil it down, my second favorite reason for using private money is that it's unlimited. When I was borrowing money from the banks, Moneeka, I had a line of credit limit. All right? And in this world of private money, there is no limit. I can do business with an unlimited number of private lenders. As I mentioned, we have 48 now. We've got about six and a half million dollars right now that we invest and move from house to house. But my absolute favorite reason for private money, Moneeka, is I receive multiple checks on every transaction and I bring no money of my own to the closings when I purchase properties.

So, how do I receive multiple checks? Well, first of all, I receive a check every time I buy a house. I mean, who doesn't want to get paid to buy houses, right? I bring none of my own money to the closing. And how does that work? Because I always borrow more than I need to buy the house. Yes, in this world of private money, the private lenders loan us more money than we need to buy the house.

Secondly, if I'm selling on rent-to-own or with a lease and an option to purchase, I'll get a nonrefundable option fee. Some people call it a lease option deposit. And then I get a third check when I cash out of the house, which is the difference between what I sell it for and what we still owe the private lender.

So, my favorite reason is receiving multiple checks on every transaction without bringing any of my own money to the close. And in fact, my favorite phrase, Moneeka, on my real estate attorney's check stub when I pick up a check says, "Excess cash to close." I always get excess cash.

Moneeka: Wow! That's amazing. Okay, so this all sounds super awesome, and I will admit that the very first time I heard this, my thought was, "Well, why would anybody want to lend to me? Why do private money lenders want to do that?" Could you address that?

Jay: Sure. There are three big reasons. First of all, they're going to earn a whole lot more money than they can through any other traditional resources. For example, let's take just a moment and talk about certificates of deposit, all right? I checked in USA Today, and as of this past Thursday, the average rate is 0.80% in a 12-month certificate of deposit. I mean, my word, we're going to have to start paying the banks to keep our money, right?

Let's say, if I come along and pay a private lender 8%. Well, 8% versus 0.8%! That's over 10 times as much in returns. If they can get 1% in a certificate of deposit, I pay them 8%, that's eight times as much money. So, number one reason is, they're going to earn a whole lot more money. Secondly, their loan to us is safe and secure. And here's how; it's safe because we don't borrow more than 75% of the **after-repair value of a property**. So, it's a conservative loan value.

And then thirdly, in my world, Moneeka, we don't borrow unsecured funds. We give all of our private lenders a mortgage in North Carolina. In some other states, it's called a deed of trust. So, we secure their note. And then fourthly—and my older private lenders love this—is that their loan amount or their principle is not volatile. Their investment is not volatile.

What I mean by that is I'm contrasting this to the stock market. If you invest in stocks or mutual funds, you've already lost money. You had to pay fees, you had to pay commissions. The value of that stock or mutual fund might be less this afternoon or tomorrow than the principal investment amount was when you started.

Well, our private lenders absolutely love that the principle loan amount remains the same until cash out. That means we are paying interest-only payments. That helps us because it helps our cash flow. And it helps our private lenders because they are earning interest on all of their principal for the entire term of the loan.

Here's how: you see, if I'm paying principal and interest down on their note, the principal amount is being paid down and they're not making as much money. Therefore, interest-only payments being paid is a win/win for both the private lender and for us.

So, three big reasons why they want to do business with us:
1) they earn a lot of money
2) it's safe and secure, and
3) the principal loan amount remains the same and it's not volatile.

Moneeka: Wow, I love that. And what I have found, because I'm actually in Jay's program, is that everything he says is true. When I present this opportunity, people look at me and say, "Wow, that's amazing." I'm loving having these conversations because I feel like I'm giving them a gift, right?

Jay: Oh, absolutely. It is a gift. Where else are your private lenders going to get these kinds of rates of return? And you know what, Moneeka, I've only received one complaint from my private lenders. Do you know what that was? They said, "Why didn't you tell me about this sooner?"

Moneeka: That's funny!

Jay: They think about the money they could have been making. So, yes, it truly is a win/win for everybody.

Moneeka: I love that. So, how do you let people know that you're offering these amazing rates of return?

Jay: I call it getting the word out. And Moneeka, since you're in my mastermind group and the platinum group and all that, you've heard me say this. I have never asked anybody for money, never. With the millions of millions of dollars that I've borrowed and done business with, I've never asked a private lender for money. I simply make my program available and get the word out.

So, how do I do that? Well, multiple ways. Moneeka, we have got a 16-minute audio called "Stress-free Investing." And that 16-minute audio gives an overview to a potential private lender as to what private money and private lending is all about. But it doesn't spill the beans. It gives an overview but it doesn't say how much interest they're going to earn, how they're protected, how they can get their money back in case of an emergency.

And so, that audio, when potential private lenders listen to it, moves them to a one-on-one with us. In the one-on-one visit, we actually do spill the beans. So, we have this audio that we can email out to potential private lenders. We have a YouTube link for it. We can text it to them. And we can hand them a CD (for anyone who still wants CDs).

We also do webinars. We invite people that are from outside our area to learn about our program. We do private lender luncheons. I have raised as much as $969,000 at one private lender luncheon. And yes, I did not ask for any money and got $969,000 in pledged funding for my deals. So, those are just a few of the ways that we're getting the word out.

Moneeka: What I really love about your system, Jay, is that we don't have to do all of those things either. We can pick one and just get really, really good at it.

Jay: Exactly. You don't have to do it all. I mean, when I raised the $2,150,000 in less than 90 days when I was cut off from the banks, all I focused on was getting the audio out. And my whole frame of mind was, I'm not chasing anybody, I'm not begging anybody, I'm not trying to talk anybody into anything. I just make the program available and those that have investment capital or retirement funds, they're going to raise their hand and they're going to want to know more.

Moneeka: Right. So, there are a lot of good reasons for them to do it. And I just love the look on people's faces when I'm talking to them about this. It's really fantastic.

And what's really cool is I've got family in Tennessee, New York, and in Texas, and they can all invest in California real estate through these programs, which they love.

So, Jay, I'm going to move into our rapid-fire questions. But before we do that, go ahead and tell my listeners a little bit about how they can get in touch with you, and this might be a nice time to introduce the live event.

Jay: Absolutely. I hold a few live events a year, and you were able to attend the last one. You were there to network with the attendees and your followers and listeners who came to the event. That's one thing about the event, the networking is phenomenal.

So, for everybody to find out when the next live event is, and if Moneeka is going to be there in person for you to meet and network with, just go to www.BlissfulPrivateMoney.com. And when Moneeka comes, typically she presents at the live event, too. So, go on over to the website at www.BlissfulPrivateMoney.com, to get all the details. (You can also get my free webinar on how to get all the private money you need to fund your deals at www.Blissfulinvestorprivatemoney.com.)

Here is an overview of the event in a nutshell. First of all, private lenders are at the event. So, you can meet and talk to my private lenders. It's got nothing to do with your credit, your income, what your hard money lender says, what your banker says. Come to the event, get the real scoop on private money. You're also going to learn how to find deals before other real estate investors even know they exist. You will also learn how to sell any house in three days or less. On the third day you will learn how to automate the business.

Moneeka: That's so cool. So, I just want to highlight a couple of things that Jay just said. First of all, private money is a really big part of his system. One of the biggest questions that I get from you, my listeners, is that you don't have the money, and that's holding you back. So, Jay has an option for us on how to get the money. But it's only one pillar of a four-pillar system that he teaches at his events. He also teaches you how to find deals for pennies on the dollar. I know that you hear this a lot, right? There are a lot of people out there saying this. But Jay has a system that's worked for him for years and that has worked consistently for his students.

The other thing I love is that he does a bus tour. So, you get to see exactly what he does. It's all real. He's not making money by selling courses. He makes his money in real estate and then sells courses because it's his passion to teach people. Jay makes his money in real estate and you get to see how.

The other thing that I really love about Jay that nobody else talks about is automation. Automation is the key to a blissful life in everything. Systems create bliss. And I know how incredibly boring that sounds, but when things flow easily because you've got everything set up in a way that you love, life is so much easier. You're not babysitting people that are tough to babysit. You're not doing things that don't make you happy. You get to stay busy in the things that bring you bliss.

So automation, first of all, it lets you stay busy in the things that bring you bliss, but it also reduces the amount of time you have to spend in this business. You all know I personally, only spend 5 to 10 hours a month in my business. How do you think I do that? It's through automation.

So, I know that it's not sexy, but I'm telling you it's the key to bliss. I just wanted to mention those things to highlight that Jay is really offering something truly amazing here. Thank you, Jay.

Jay: Hey, thank you so much, Moneeka. And I can't wait 'til the next event.

Moneeka: Me too! Okay, so here are our three rapid-fire questions. Are you ready?

Jay: I've got my seatbelt on.

Moneeka: Okay, so tell us one strategy on getting started in real estate investing.

Jay: Just remember that the money comes first. And let me explain what I mean by the money comes first. Here's the thing. Most sellers will not sell to us creatively. They require all the money. They won't sell to us with seller financing, give us an option, or sell subject to the existing note. They want all the money. And guess what? When we don't have the money lined up, i.e. private money, we're missing out on most of the opportunities.

So, starting out, my advice is focus on getting the funding first, and then you don't have to worry about missing out on deals. Because here's the thing: there are always deals. Don't worry about getting these lead sheets figured out. Get the funding lined up, and then you'll never miss out on a deal because you didn't have the money.

Moneeka: The thing is that a lot of sellers just get confused when you talk about all these other creative financing options. I've talked to realtors and even they got confused. But everyone understands cash.

Jay: Moneeka, that reminds me. One reason that I get more deals accepted from listings on the multiple listing service or from for sale by owners is that in my offers I put that I can close with no contingencies within seven days!

Moneeka: Wow!

Jay: Many times another real estate investor will have another offer in. They may even offer more money than me. But because I can close within seven days with no contingencies, I get more deals accepted.

Moneeka: I love that. So, tell us one super tip on being successful in real estate investing.

Jay: Until you own the real estate between your ears, it will be very difficult for you to own dirt real estate. What I'm talking about is being in control of your life. So, how do you do that? How do you balance all areas of your life? Your spiritual side, financial side, career side, personal relationships, etc? One particular daily habit that I have, I learned from Hal Elrod, who wrote Miracle Morning. He has a morning ritual that he teaches that I have just subscribed to. And the acronym is SAVERS. That stands for Silence, Affirmations, Visualization, Exercise, Reading, and Scribing or Journaling.

I know that sounds like a lot, but that miracle morning that Hal Elrod talks about can just set your day up for success, no matter what you're doing.

Moneeka: Great! You actually answered the last question that I was going to ask, too, which was about a daily practice that contributes to your personal success. Thank you for that. And I just want to say that in my book Choose Bliss, which is really about creating a life of bliss, I also cover the morning routine. Because whether it's in your business or it's in your life, if you haven't grounded yourself, if you haven't decided to be joyful for this experience of a new day, everything is going to come AT you rather than you going to it from a place of joy, acceptance, and openness so that miracles can happen.

For me, too, that's a really important strategy that I've taught my coaching clients for many years. And it's also covered in my book, Choose Bliss. So, thank you so much for bringing that up because not many people talk about it. Only the very, very successful people seem to know about this strategy.

Jay, thank you so much for sharing all of your wisdom with my listeners today. Thanks for being on the show.

Jay: Absolutely. Thank you for having me, Moneeka. I always enjoy it. And again, looking forward to the upcoming live event.

> *"Successes are not an accident. If you want anything*
> *worthwhile to come about, get on your calendar now*
> *to plan and implement. Successes are scheduled!"*
> ~JAY CONNER

FIND A WAY TO PAY OFF YOUR DEBTS
WITH MARK WILLIS

Moneeka: Today, I'd like to welcome to our show Mark Willis. Mark is a man on a mission to help you think differently about banks, Wall Street, and financial uncertainty.

After graduating with six figures of student loan debt and discovering a way to turn his debt into real wealth and watching everybody lose their retirement investments and home equity in 2008, he knew that he needed to find a sane way to meet his financial objectives and those of his clients.

Mark is a CFP® / CERTIFIED FINANCIAL PLANNER™, a #1 bestselling author, and the owner of Lake Growth Financial Services, a financial firm in Chicago, Illinois. Over the years, he has helped hundreds of his clients take back control of their financial future and build their businesses with sophisticated tax-efficient financial solutions. He specializes in building custom-tailored financial strategies that are unknown to typical financial gurus.

A cohost of the Not Your Average Financial Podcast™, he shares some of his strategies for investing in real estate, saving and paying for college without going broke, and creating an income in retirement you can't outlive. Mark works with people who want to grow their wealth in ways that are safe and predictable, to become their own source of financing and to create tax-free income in retirement.

Yay! Hello, Mark. Welcome to the show.

Mark: So glad to be on. Thanks, Moneeka.

Moneeka: Could you start by just giving us a little bit more of your story. I know you've got a daughter, your wife is involved in the financial industry—so give us a little bit more about who you are.

Mark: I love having this life. It's a great life. We are living in incredible times. We have such an opportunity to participate in the real estate space, to be your own boss. And for me, it was a passion around numbers. I guess I was a nerd after all, and I never was told that.

But yeah, the story starts after getting out of college. We did have six figures in student loan debt in the midst of the great recession. It was 2008 when I got out of g rad school. And we had no plan, Moneeka, for how to pay that monster of a debt off. I mean, the monthly payments alone were like a mortgage payment to us. My wife and I said it almost felt like we had this chain around our necks. And yeah, it was in the midst of 2008, not really a great time to be looking for work right out of college.

Moneeka: I can relate.

Mark: All of my training, however, was in mutual funds, stock market—just buy them and hope and pray that the stock market will always go up. And I listened to the likes of financial info-tainers on the radio like Mr. Dave Ramsey and other friends. And we were plowing everything we could into our student loan payments. And we were feeling good about our rice and beans every night that we were eating for dinner. I mean, that was sort of our life for a few years there.

And we never really stopped to think about the cost of paying off our debt. A lot of folks have asked me what's the biggest financial mistake I've ever made. And I would say that it's going broke paying off our debts, which sounds sort of like a counterintuitive comment.

But it wasn't until a mentor of mine came to visit my wife Katrina and I, and shared this strategy that we call "Bank On Yourself®" that a light bulb went off. And we started thinking, "Well, wow, wait a minute, we are essentially slaves to our debt. We're slaves to the bank. And every dollar that we throw at our debt is a dollar we'll never see again. And not only will we not see that dollar ever again when we give it, we'll never see what that dollar could have done for us over our lifetime." Because a dollar today might grow to 7, 9, 10 dollars in the future.

So we started putting those numbers together on top of the debt that we currently owed, and that was a ton of cash. I mean, that's like a retirement account plus. And so we ended up getting so interested in our own finances that we got our own money straight and we opened up a practice in the midst of the great recession to say, "Here are some strategies and here are some concepts and here's a mindset for being better than debt-free." But actually becoming our own banker, becoming our own source of financing to help folks like myself and my wife not only break free from debt, but actually control the financial environment where our money lives.

So whether it's a student loan that we're trying to pay off, a credit card, or a mortgage on some investment properties, we've been passionate about getting the word out that there is something out there that's better than debt-free, better than just saving as being a wealth accumulator.

Moneeka: Wow! So my head just blew up. You just said everything against what I believe. I can't wait to further this conversation. So let's dig a little deeper on kind of what's wrong with the traditional financial planning model.

Mark: Well, again, I've been classically trained as a CFP® / CERTIFIED FINANCIAL PLANNER™. Everything they really present in our training and education, I took whole-heartedly—that the White Knight of Wall Street was going to come in and rescue us. But that isn't the case. If you look over the last 30 years (this is independent research by DALBAR, the quantitative analysis of investment behavior), their annual study of real actual investors before taxes and before fees (this shocked me) shows the average return was only 3.6% in the stock markets. And that includes the 1990s bull market, and our massive bull market in the last 10 years. And we've come up with a whopping 3.6% real return. And that's before taxes and before investment fees.

So we're hardly even keeping up with inflation in the stock market, and yet that's the only thing anyone ever tells us to do with our money. If we have 50 bucks to our name, most investment advisors will tell you to throw it into a brokerage account or a 401k. So, I was surprised when I learned this information.

It's like there's only one thing on their menu, and they can chop it up in multiple different ways, but it's the same answer. And that is Wall Street, Wall Street, and more Wall Street.

We had to be woken up, I suppose, to the truth about Wall Street. It's not written on any stone tablet or there's no law that says we have to throw all of our money into Wall Street to get to financial independence.

So it was sort of that moment when I realized, "Wow, wait a minute, I've been throwing all of my money into a hole, which is our debt. And I've been hoping and praying that our rate of return would be higher so we could somehow someday get to a place where we can comfortably retire."

So what's wrong with traditional financial planning? I think it's the myth of what's known as average rates of return. We can talk about that if you'd like. It's that fees on our investments are usually gobbling up on average, according to the Department of Labor, about a third of our life savings. So if you have a 1% fee on your portfolio, that's one third of your money gone over a 30-year period. 37% specifically according to the Department of Labor. Can you imagine?

Moneeka: It's just painful, my goodness.

Mark: Can you imagine?

Moneeka: No, actually, I can't.

Mark: Yeah. I mean, think about that. For the average person, that's a six-figure lump sum going to an investment advisor, and he or she is going to get paid on your account whether the market is up, down, or sideways. They get a guaranteed chunk of your cash every single year. We the investors, don't have any kind of guarantee.

Moneeka: And a lot of that is not even disclosed. It kind of becomes invisible.

Mark: Right. And then, really, it becomes a problem when it comes time to retire. I started thinking about this, too. What is an investment advisor's incentive to help you spend your money in retirement? As you're spending down the assets that are under their management, they're being paid less and less and less because there's less and less to manage, as you're getting into your 60s, 70s, and 80s.

So they're not going to be returning your calls. They're not going to give you a full comprehensive financial plan to spend down your money, if they're busy helping other folks who are still accumulating money. Retirement the most crucial part of your financial life. If you think about it, most people have a financial plan that's all about accumulate, accumulate, accumulate. But the goal of climbing a mountain is not to get to the top, in my opinion, it's to come back down safely.

85% of deaths on Mount Everest happen while coming down the mountain. And yes, the top is fun. It's a great view. But if my mountain-climbing Sherpa assistant said, "You know what, you're on your own, buddy, for the way down," I would be in big trouble. Most investment advisors don't have a clue and don't have a plan to help you spend the money you've accumulated in a way that won't make you run out of cash.

I feel like real estate is a great way to help solve that problem because that renter is going to give you that check for as long as you hold your property. I think there's other financial products and strategies that don't run out of cash, even if you run out of money. Like annuities, for example, are a great one for that. Pensions are another great one, as rare as they are these days.

But I think in terms of traditional financial planning, they don't have a plan. And how can we call it "financial planning" if there's no plan for how much you're going to have at retirement, how much you can spend as you go into retirement, and how long that money will last? It's all a big weather forecast, and they have no control over any of it.

Moneeka: It's so interesting because I do talk to a lot of people that are saying, "Well, I've been investing in my 401k, I've been investing in my ESPP, and I hope that I'll have enough." And the thing is that hope is not a financial plan, right?

Mark: I'm clapping, yes.

Moneeka: A **plan** is a financial plan. And you bring up some really good points that even I hadn't thought about. Because I've been in the accumulation phase, and I have often thought David and I would just self-fund. We're not going to be dependent. We've built our real estate portfolio, we've been very active with our mutual funds and our stock. We've got a diversified plan.

So I sort of feel like we are handled because we're both really financially involved. Most people don't have the time or the interest to spend on that. We're kind of numbers geeks, right?

Mark: That's right. We're hanging out.

Moneeka: And even us with as much as we know, I had never really thought through those pieces because they're far away. When you get to the top of the mountain, when you're coming back down, well, that has been kind of far away, so I haven't thought about that. So, such good points. Thank you for that.

Mark: Yeah, you want to pack enough food, so to speak, to not only get to the top of your mountain but to come back down safely and plant your flag safely and securely back down at home base. I feel like that's the best thing to do.

And good for you for paying attention to your financial life. I do think that it does take some more intentionality. Unfortunately, I feel like most people, they get the 401k when they get their day job and they never think about it again for 30, 40 years, and none of this occurs to them. And then all of a sudden, they've got $250,000 to $500,000 in their 401k. They've got most of their money in their house, they have no guaranteed income stream of any kind. And now, they've got to figure out, "What do I do with this half million bucks in a 401k so I don't run out of income before I run out of birthday candles?"

Moneeka: Unless they're listening to this podcast . . .

Mark: Unless they're listening, yes, amen!

Moneeka: A lot of my ladies are thinking about it.

Mark: Good for you, guys. That's awesome! Keep it up.

Moneeka: So talk to me about your point of view on ROI. I know you've got a different definition for it.

Mark: Yeah, ROI normally means "return on investment." And again, I would say that average returns mean nothing. First, I want to dispel the myth that average returns of the stock market have been 10% a year. We've already talked about real investor returns were closer to 3.6% according to third-party analysis.

Now, I want to talk about why averages don't mean a thing. Let me give you a quick math example, and I'll try to keep this simple. So let's imagine that you had $10,000, and let's say that you were able to double your money in the first year. And that means you went from $10,000 up to $20,000 and you doubled your money. That's 100% rate of return. Sound good so far?

Moneeka: Sounds good.

Mark: And then in year two, we have $20,000 we're starting out with, but now we lose half your life savings, not good, right? That's a negative 50% in year two. Now let's total it up. We went from 20,000 (cut it in half), we're back down to our original $10,000. Over the two years, 100% rate of return in the first year minus the 50% in year two, that is an average rate of return, Moneeka, of 25% over two years: (100-50)/2=25.

So I just gave you an average rate of return of 25%. Don't you feel great? I mean, you've got 25% average rate of return, right?

Moneeka: Oh, what an amazing way to look at that. Because with your numbers, you're still at $10,000. You're right back where you started, but with a 25% ROI in the traditional sense.

Mark: You're right back where you started. The average return means nothing. I mean, think of it this way, if I told you that the river in your town was an average of five feet deep, would you feel comfortable walking through that river?

Moneeka: No.

Mark: I would not. If I couldn't swim, I would not feel good because averages don't account for volatility. And that's the real missing piece. And what's so crucial here, Moneeka, is that mutual funds are allowed to advertise average rates of return, which means nothing for the likes of you and me who are just trying to figure out how much more money do I have this year than I had last year.

For your listeners that are really wanting to geek out on the numbers, check out the internal rate of return or the compound annual growth rate. For the folks that really want to go deep into that, that's the right thing to look at. The compound annual growth rate is the true return, the increased dollars that you've received year over year over year. Most mutual funds won't tell you that, or at least you won't find it on their brochures, that's for sure.

Moneeka: That's right. So interesting.

Mark: But, rate of return is one way to look at it. My belief is we want a rate of income (my version of ROI). I want a check in the mail every month. And what is the rate of the income that I'll receive? That's my ROI. I'm looking for how much money will it take for me to generate a paycheck that I could never outlive and, in fact, would begin to continue to increase over my retirement years to help keep up with inflation.

Moneeka: So I just want to interject here, ladies. ROI, we normally think of return on investment. And what Mark is saying is that he looks at ROI as rate of income. So return on investment versus rate of income. And I love what you're talking about with the rate of income because that's really the endgame. We need to know what we make on that money and if it's not going to pay us.

Mark: Right. Well, even with real estate, even with stocks, there's really no return, it's just a change in the value. Until somebody sells that property, an investment is only worth what someone is willing to pay for it. Until then, all you have are paper profits.

Moneeka: Or paper losses.

Mark: Or paper losses, exactly.

Moneeka: You don't lose money until you sell, either.

Mark: That's right, that's true. It's all about what someone's willing to pay you for it when it's time to sell. That's the return of your investment. Until then, it's just a change on a sheet of paper, for sure. And it's all about in the meantime, how much cash flow can we get off of those tenants or off of that property or dividends off of that stock? Until then, that's the only thing that matters is the cash flow that comes from your holdings, your portfolio.

Moneeka: Good. So what are some core questions you ask clients when they come to you wanting to put together a portfolio?

Mark: Some of the key questions are, "What do you want your money to do for you?" At the end of the day, I can't recommend something until I know what they are looking for. What is their personal outcome? "What do you see happening with taxes?" For example. "Is it okay to pay 1% a year to an investment advisor of your whole net worth, or 2%, depending on the portfolio, or 3%? What do you think about the access to the money? Do you want access to that money before you're 59 and a half years old? Do you want to have a low cost accessibility of the money? Do you want that money to be open and available for creditors if you were to go through a bankruptcy?"

Real estate investors and listeners to the show, I'm sure you all know that it's not if you are faced with a lawsuit, but a matter of when. Typically, over the course of a real estate investor's lifetime, four lawsuits is the average.

So it's about how do we protect the other money that's not tied up in properties. So that when you go through an unfortunate event like a lawsuit, how do we keep those dollars off the radar of the courts?

So these are the questions that I'd want to ask clients and sit down with them and just figure out. Most people have an idea, but they've never been asked the question, "What do you truly want your money to do for you?" A hedge fund makes your money act different than, say, a savings account would or an annuity would or a piece of real estate would.

And it's about building (as you said earlier, Moneeka) a diversified platform to grow a true pyramid of financial wealth from the base all the way up to the top, and allocating accordingly.

Moneeka: It is interesting because the big question that I've always asked is about liquidity. And you talked about this. But for you, it is just one of the pieces of the puzzle. So for me, I know that my real estate really isn't liquid. That's for the future. And then I have my other money growing so that it's more liquid to compensate if I have to put some more money in, like I did to hold onto my real estate in 2008. Or if there's an emergency, or there's a big expenditure coming up.

So that's what we thought about. But we haven't thought about these other pieces. So I'm glad that you ask those questions right up front about all of those pieces of the puzzle.

Mark: Let's do a thought experiment. Imagine if you could be the pope of money for the day. If you could just wave a magic wand and create a perfect financial vehicle, what kind of characteristics would you want it to have? I ask that to a lot of folks. And obviously, some of the first things they say, is they want a good solid rate of return. They want it to be available for them anytime they want, like you said—liquidity or accessibility of the cash. They don't want penalties and taxes to get money out of their investment.

They usually want some sort of predictable growth of the money, something that they can count on, like we talked about, a plan. They usually don't want a big, hefty expense or fee to manage this thing. They usually want it to be, again, protected from credit risk and a predator risk. They typically want it to be available in retirement tax-free, and they typically want some sort of management to pass it on to a future generation.

And they want all of those things in a way that doesn't give half of it to the IRS. So those are the usual answers I hear from folks. I don't know if you have any feedback or would add anything to that.

Moneeka: No, actually, that was a great rundown. And those are similar questions to what my parents have been asking, what I am asking now, those sorts of things. So that's really good.

I want to move on to this concept that you have about banking on yourself. I love the way that you phrase that, and I want to hear more about what that means.

Mark: Well, it's a book that was written by Pamela Yellen a few years ago. And funny enough, as I was going through my CFP®, I'd never heard of this concept. But you can do this as an individual, you don't need 200 million bucks to go out and start an FDIC insured bank here, you can literally be your own source of financing for the small stuff of life, your vacations, your property taxes, your cars, your kids' education. You can become your own banker when it comes to your own real estate purchases.

So I have many of our clients who are literally using their own banking system to purchase real estate and cutting out the mortgage companies, cutting out the private money lenders, cutting out the outside financing, and literally putting the money they would have sent to a mortgage down the street into their own pockets for their own financial future and the future of their kids and grandkids as well.

And it's using a very old financial vehicle. And when I first heard about this vehicle, I was very skeptical at first. It's using a modernized form of this 200-year-old vehicle that has grown guaranteed every single year. It's using a whole life insurance contract, paid with dividends. In fact, it really hits everything that I just listed in that list of characteristics just a minute ago.

Whole life insurance does that. It's available to you tax-free. You can get access to the money in about three to five business days. It grows on a guaranteed basis every single year, no matter what's going on in the stock market. I mean, while not guaranteed, the insurance companies who offer these exclusive contracts have paid dividends into these policies every year for the last century, including during the Great Depression. You can get the money out tax-free and you can even pass it onto your kids, totally income tax-free. So it fits a lot of the boxes for using the policy for the function of banking in your life.

So before we get into the product and vehicle, I'll just say it does require a new way of thinking, Moneeka. It takes learning to think like a banker, to see yourself as the banker on the other side of the desk. Usually, we're sitting on the borrowing side. But to think like a banker is to change your mind and change how you see yourself. But yeah, using this policy lets you borrow money from the policy, like a line of credit to yourself. It's a big pool of contingency cash. If you've got 100, 200, 500,000, a million dollars in cash value in this policy, you can then use that as capital for your real estate needs or for your kids college, or for anything else you might want—cars, vacations, whatever. And it just works and it continues to grow even on that capital that you've borrowed out.

So it sort of allows your money to do two things at once, which I think solves some of the problems that many real estate investors I come across are stuck in. Which is access to capital.

What's that old quote from Mark Twain? He says "A banker is a fellow who will lend you his umbrella when the sun is shining, but wants it back as soon as it starts to rain." He's awesome! I love that guy. I love it.

Moneeka: My last name's Sawyer—I'm a particular fan.

Mark: Beautiful, I like that. Nice! Any relation?

Moneeka: No, but my father-in-law is Tom Sawyer.

Mark: Is that right? Wow, that's amazing!

Moneeka: He's not the original, but that's his name. It's really kind of funny.

Mark: Love that.

Well, so think of it this way. Imagine if you had a permanent line of credit that you got the interest on, and you were able to use that for real estate in good times and bad. So, when the banks stop lending again, and when the lines of credit are called and taken away, which real estate investors will be most ready to take advantage of the next recession? It'll be the folks with big piles of contingency cash for the opportunities that present themselves. And for many of our clients, who do have significant wealth in some of these policies, it's this wealth that they'll be drawing on to pay cash for real estate purchases.

Moneeka: So I have to confess, I'm very skeptical on this. So I would love to dive deeper, but we don't have all the time to do that right now. So tell me who this is a good fit for and who it's not a good fit for. Let's start there.

Mark: Moneeka, believe me, I was just as skeptical. As soon as I heard the words " whole life insurance" the alarm bells started going off and my mind shut off. Thank goodness I didn't get stuck in analysis paralysis. But it did take me about seven months to overcome my own bias. And here I was a CFP® and should have known better, but I was working on the investment track. I was helping clients out of the worst recession since the Great Depression. And I guess I was sort of watching the house of cards of real estate and Wall Street come tumbling down.

So maybe that experience helped me sort of open my mind some. I would not recommend anyone just hop into any old whole life insurance policy. Most whole life out there is going to grow very slowly and not have any cash value in the first five or six years, give or take.

So you don't want to just hop into any old policy. Honestly, the shortest answer I can give you is to work with a competent advisor who's been trained in the concept of "Bank On Yourself," and work with someone who is willing to take a huge pay cut. Roughly about 70% of their commissions has to be forfeited, which is why as a CFP® I'm really proud to represent that strategy because I do think it's in the client's best interest to not take giant commissions off a policy like most investment advisors who do wealth management and investment planning. Because those commissions are cut, Moneeka, the vast majority of your contribution or premium into the policy is available to you right away.

So unlike old-fashioned whole life, which our parents probably had or grandparents might have had, it's been modernized to be a lot more efficient. You get cash value in the first month, in the first year, first few years, and it's available to you to use for real estate or other needs right from the start. So that's the shortest answer in the time we have.

I remember when my mentor shared this strategy with me, he asked me as my brow was furrowed and my arms were crossed . . . he said, "Mark, is it possible that Dave Ramsey could be wrong about something?" And he just let that question hang in the air. And for me, I had never considered that. But I'm sure for many of your listeners who are more critical thinkers than I was at the time, they may have already figured out that Dave Ramsey may not have actually written the 10 commandments of finance.

But you're right, if you have an open mind, I'd say it's worth investigating. It's not a good fit for folks who would prefer to use other people's money. It does take saving. Over time, you do get a significant accumulation inside the policy, but you will still need to save. So living within your means is a requirement. It's also never going to be a 30% rate of return. It's going to be a steady cash equivalent; I've seen it somewhere between 4 and 7% after taxes. So not too shabby.

Moneeka: Hold on, so that's 4 to 7% after tax?

Mark: Correct, yeah.

Moneeka: So this is not apples to apples, right? Because you usually hear 4-7%, but that's before taxes. Usually when you hear that, you assume that amount will get taxed later.

Mark: That's right. Very observant. Yeah, you're right. If an investment is doing 8 or 9%, then after tax it might be only doing 4 or 5%. You're right.

So given all that, I would say take a look at it. Don't put ALL your money into something like this. And make sure you talk to an advisor who knows what he or she is doing when putting it together for you. That's the most important thing I could say in our short conversation.

Moneeka: So we have a lot of younger women in my audience. We also have some older women like myself. And one of the concerns that I'm having jump into my mind right now is, if whole life is actually a life insurance policy (and I don't know that much about it), premiums are going to be significantly higher for someone like me than a younger woman. Is that true?

Mark: Well, the way we would design it is very different from focusing on the death benefit. So yes, all things considered, someone who's 19 years old is going to cost less to the insurance company than a 69-year-old or a 79-year-old. But the way we design it, it's really all about how much can I squeeze into this policy for the least amount of death benefit. We're cutting out all the expenses and commissions because the main focus of the policy is the cash accumulation. How much liquidity can we have in the first year?

With term insurance, the mindset is like renting an apartment. You want to pay as little for rent as possible. When you own this policy that's going to build wealth for you, it's all about, "How much equity can I build up in this policy?" Sort of like owning a piece of real estate. "So how much can I pack into this policy with as few expenses as I possibly can?"

And again, the purpose of the cash value is to keep it in motion, to use it right away. So for folks that are 29 years old or 49 years old or 69 years old, the death benefit will be higher or lower, but the cash value should accumulate roughly the same.

Moneeka: Interesting, I love that. Thank you.

Now, why don't you tell my audience how they can get in touch with you to talk about all this stuff? Because there's probably many questions out there.

Mark: Yeah, it really complements the real estate portfolio. Again, I'd say maybe 40 to 50% of our clients are in the real estate investment space. Using these strategies is a part of a comprehensive financial plan that we would set up for folks. Again, it's one strategy we specialize in; it's not the only thing we do.

So the best way you can learn more about this concept is to check out our podcast. If you love Moneeka's awesome show—and I love your show by the way, it's awesome.

Moneeka: Yay, thank you.

Mark: If you want to go deeper down this rabbit hole, check out our show. It's called Not Your Average Financial Podcast™. Or go to our website AmazingWomeninRealEstate.com and click "request a free analysis ." We can chat for 15 minutes just one on one. Happy to do that.

And if you'd like, just put Moneeka's name in the notes of the event, and I'll be sure to send you a copy of our bestselling book at no charge at all, as long as you're in the United States. If you're outside of the United States, I'll give you a PDF.

Moneeka: Tell us the name of the book, I love it.

Mark: Oh, it's really how the same strategy works for ecommerce businesses. If you have an online business, the same concepts hold true. You need to buy inventory, you need to recycle capital. So the book title is How to Be an Amazon Legend and Fire Your Banker!

Moneeka: I just love that. Okay, great. So, Mark, are you ready for our three rapid-fire questions?

Mark: Let's do it.

Moneeka: So start by just telling us a super tip on getting started investing in real estate.

Mark: Find one person like Moneeka, who you can trust and just follow everything she says. Don't get too many mentors, just find one or maybe two. But then just put all your efforts into just following their system. Because if you get too many voices in your head, it gets confusing. But just get one or two and then go after it. But put yourself to work, and it'll start to work. It's a downhill slope and you start to pick up momentum really fast.

Moneeka: Nice. And then what is one strategy on being successful in real estate investing?

Mark: I do think that there's a lot of good in putting your trust in other people. But at the end of the day, it is, "What do you find that you're most passionate about?" Because if you are being told to get into multifamily and you're all about storage units, then you're going to have a hard time getting passionate about someone else's passion.

So find what you're really into, what you're really focused on. What do you find yourself just reading about on the weekends? What do you find yourself just perusing YouTube to learn more about? And then just go into that, and be okay with being weird because that's what makes you, you.

Moneeka: I love that. And that's such a big deal because there are so many voices. And a confused mind can't decide. And if you go after somebody else's good idea that doesn't settle with you, it's just not going to work long-term. You're going to burn out. So I love that advice. Thank you for that.

What would you say is one daily practice you do, Mark, that contributes to your personal success?

Mark: Man, Audible is awesome. We're living in the future, Moneeka, I'm telling you. It's so cool. We get to listen to the voices of people who've given their lives to some topic or idea or strategy. I mean, come on, we're living in this incredible age where we have at our fingertips the wisdom of thousands of years, and we can never take it all in, in our lifetime.

So yeah, taking a little bit of time to learn. For me, usually it's after dinner when we're cleaning up the house, my daughter's put down to bed—I'll listen to some Audible every day. And that's been a lot of fun. Just try to get into reading, or at least listening to books. As a busy parent, that's an important practice. No matter how busy we are, we can always find time to listen to an audible book, is my opinion.

Moneeka: I love that. So you're constantly learning.

Mark: Yes, it's the best way to put your dishwashing time to work for you.

Moneeka: Exactly. And I actually just found out that you can go onto the Amazon Echo and say, "Alexa, play real estate investing for women," and it will fill up your house.

Mark: Wow, I had no idea. That's cool.

Moneeka: You can do this for lots of things. There are resources for us to have access to learning that are so easy. You don't have to download it all. There's all these different ways to do this. It's so awesome, I love it.

Mark: Oh, good.

Moneeka: So Mark, thank you so much for sharing all of this great information and really making me think on some new concepts. I definitely want to dive deeper on that. Thank you so much for coming on and sharing all this with us.

> *"If you control the environment where your money lives, you win. If banks control the environment where your money lives, they win."*
> ~ NELSON NASH

5 POWER PILLARS OF SELF-DIRECTED INVESTING
EVERY WOMAN SHOULD KNOW
WITH AMANDA HOLBROOK

Moneeka: Today, I am delighted to introduce you to our guest Amanda Holbrook.

Amanda has been a passionate driving force in the world of self-directed IRAs for 10 years and running. Her experience in the self-directed and non-traditional investing arenas allows her to add remarkable value to all of the families and businesses that she works with as VP at Specialized Trust Company. She has the ability to really connect and simplify self-directed concepts so that anyone can apply it in their own financial lives. Even her young children self-direct!

Amanda is a proud mother of two, loving wife, self-directed IRA ninja, and active investor, in that order.

Hi there, Amanda, how are you?

Amanda: Hello Moneeka, thank you so much for having me on today.

Moneeka: I'll start by asking you what are the top three obstacles to financial freedom most people face?

Amanda: The first obstacle for folks when it comes to financial freedom is they simply fail to plan. Just one ounce of prevention is all it takes. If you fail to plan, you plan to fail. That can be applied to anything from our personal relationships, to our weight, and our personal finances are no different. This is the number one obstacle I see for both families and businesses. Start with your vision, your ideal life, and build from there. Everyone is different in this respect.

Do you know the number one piece of feedback we hear repeatedly? Whether it's after a personal conversation, a podcast, or having heard our team speak at a seminar, it is always the same. "I wish they would have heard about this 10, 15, 20 years ago." I cannot tell you how many baby boomers and those who are already in retirement I hear this from on a weekly basis. There are a multitude of paths to financial freedom. Not all of them have to be via the stock market. Welcome to the wonderful world of self-direction.

The second obstacle is making a plan but not taking action. First, kudos to you if you are listening to this podcast, absorbing books, taking courses, attending events, and soaking in the knowledge of other experts in the field in order to better yourself and your families' futures. What you focus on, you find. Pat yourself on the back. Now here's the obstacle, NOT taking action. I've heard this put various ways over the years. Some a bit more bluntly than others, so hopefully this is a good reminder. **Education without execution is just entertainment.** I've seen some pretty expensive entertainment out there in this arena. TAKE ACTION.

The third obstacle we see most is not having a rock-solid team. This goes back to planning, but there is no one who has true success without a team behind them. The same rules that apply to our personal lives and businesses, also apply to our financial health, success, and overall bliss.

Think of it this way, ladies: you don't choose your doctor because she's conveniently located next to your mani/pedi/hair salon. Same can be said about your financial team. Do not limit yourself to geography or convenience. Surround yourself with excellence. Strive to not be the smartest person in the room and then get the right butts in the right seats. There is no polite way to say that. I don't care if you are building your own financial roundtable or your business. You have to have the right butts in the right seats. Credit to Traction by Gino Wickman if you have not read it. Once established, you need to evaluate that team as you grow, things change, and goals change. Just because your family has used XYZ financial professional for XYZ years does not mean that person will always be a fit for you. Those are the top three obstacles.

Moneeka: Thank you for that. Could you define self-direction?

Amanda: Sure thing, Moneeka. A self-directed IRA is just that, an IRA that YOU self-direct, or any self-directed account, for that matter. Most people will read this and think, "well, I have a self-directed IRA/401(k) already." You would not be alone. Is it truly self-directed? Many big box companies, that I'm not going to name, have YOU log on to your account, YOU pick your stock/bond/mutual fund, therefore YOU are self-directing. They tell you it's a self-directed IRA. It says that right on the screen. It must be a self-directed IRA, right? WRONG! But YOU get to pick the stock/bond/mutual fund yourself, so it must be. That is NOT what self-direction is, Moneeka, and everyone listening out there. I cannot stress that enough.

A true self-directed IRA allows you to invest in opportunities outside of the stock market. Plus you are not limited to just personal IRAs when it comes to self-direction. There are also HSAs, Roth IRAs, Roth 401(k)s, Coverdell Educational accounts for kids. Get that IRA stigma out of your head. Self-directed accounts allow you to invest in non-traditional assets. Basically anything that is outside of the stock market, within the parameters the IRS sets, is fair game. For example: real estate, rental properties, tax liens, private lending, private companies, livestock, apartment syndications, timber, equipment leasing, etc. These are examples of non-traditional, self-directed investments. You are only limited by your own creativity.

Moneeka: Wow!

Amanda: Yeah!

Moneeka: Oh, my goodness! You just turned IRAs into a really fascinating thing. The control is really exciting.

Amanda: Absolutely. It's fun, it's sexy. I'm going to make it even simpler because I hate jargon. Self-directed accounts simply allow you to take what YOU know, YOUR personal expertise, and apply it to YOUR retirement account; that's it.

If you breed cattle in Texas, we can show you that you can breed cattle in your retirement account. That is absolutely possible! I know that these are one-off scenarios for most listening, but that's the absolute beauty of it. Moneeka, were you born and raised to know how to buy, sell, and trade stock?

Moneeka: No.

Amanda: No, none of us were. With today's education, we are not taught that in high school. That is another passion of mine we will not get into now. Financially educating our youth has to be a priority. Today, we're going to start with the parents.

Moneeka: Yes, that's awesome and I'm totally with you on that.

You said something briefly earlier that I want to go back to about self-direction: it can be an IRA, but you mentioned some other different kinds of accounts, like the HSA, the medical money accounts, are there any other kind of accounts that you can use?

Amanda: Sure. The question I get a lot is "how do I get an account that is self-directed?" It always seems to be a mystery, yet it is easy. I want to reiterate that you can self-direct the following type of accounts: Roth IRAs, which is number one. Everyone should have a Roth IRA, even your kids. More on that in a moment. Traditional IRAs, health savings accounts (HSAs), Coverdell Educational Savings accounts, SEP IRAs, SIMPLE IRAs, Solo-401(k) s, Roth Solo 401(k)s. If you have a TSP, 403(b), Pension Plan, 401(k)—these plans can be moved to self-directed plans.

We all have health insurance, and a high deductible per the IRS is only $2,700 per family this year. This is one of my favorites, Moneeka. You can have your cake and eat it too. Meaning the funds you put in are tax-deferred, but it grows tax-free like a Roth does. If you have an HSA you can self-direct it. An HSA is a big one when it comes to long-term care. Imagine having rental income within an HSA taking care of your long-term health costs. That takes the burden off your personal finances or your loved ones. There are 10,000 baby boomers retiring a day. This is the current reality.

With a Coverdell educational savings accounts, you can pay for your child's K-12 education as well as higher ed, and you can transfer them from child to child to child as they get older.

There are SEP IRAs, SIMPLE IRAs. If you are an entrepreneurial woman, the BEST account in my opinion is a Roth Solo 401(k.)

The whole point of self-direction, Moneeka, is taking control of your financial future. With a self-directed account, guess who is in control? It's in the name: yourself.

Moneeka: This is so fascinating because I have many different accounts, sort of all over the place, and it would be fun to consolidate them and then take control of where I invest; that is really exciting. Why don't we hear about this stuff, because it's not out there? Right?

Amanda: A question I hear all of the time, "Why haven't I heard of this before?" The reason why you don't hear about it from the big bank down the street or the broker who manages your family assets is because it's not profitable for them. For Specialized Trust Company, this is our niche. We are a boutique financial firm, and we are a passive custodian. That is our role. A passive custodian means we do not recommend or endorse specific investments. We are not CPAs, so we give no tax advice. We are not attorneys, so we don't give legal advice. We are a crucial member of your financial team because we have no self-serving agenda for us in the relationship. Why don't the big guys on Wall Street offer this? Because it's a financial burden to them, one. It's an administrative burden, two. And it's not profitable enough for them, three.

There are reasons you are pushed toward certain mutual funds at one institution and a different set at another. Because there is a monetary back-end incentive for them. That is how Wall Street works.

In self-direction, the fees are very transparent, so you know what you are paying up front as one should. Over the hundreds of events I've presented in over the years, no one can ever tell me exactly what fees they pay for their retirement account because no one knows unless it's self-directed. For the average American, their second largest asset is their retirement account. This is second only to their primary home. Why don't you know? You could likely tell me what you paid for your car, but not your retirement account. Why? That needs to change. The average account holder is paying 6-7% in fees and has no clue.

With us, if you are investing in a rental property in your own town, for example, there is no backend profit for the passive custodian. It is completely up to you what to invest in. As I said earlier, we are passive. We support YOU with education, service, and experience so YOU can be in control of YOUR financial future. That is the whole point.

Self-directed accounts are regulated per the IRS just like all other retirement accounts. Feel free to read publications 590-A, 590-B, IRC 4975, and more. My point here is if you plug "IRS FAQs" in your search engine, you will see it there in black and white. Trustees are not required to offer real estate as an option, but it is not prohibited. That means you can narrow the lines you are allowed to color within, but no one is allowed to color outside the lines.

Moneeka: Interesting. Can anyone do self-directed accounts? Are there any restrictions on that?

Amanda: Absolutely. You need a social security number, earned income, and a heartbeat.

Moneeka: That's it? Okay, earned income: that can be from a business, W-2, or contracts?

Amanda: Yes; from W-2 or 1099 derived from a service provided.

Moneeka: Awesome. Let's jump into real estate. How does that hold with investing in real estate in a self-directed IRA?

Amanda: Great loaded question. Real estate is one of my categories when it comes to any tax-sheltered self-directed accounts. There are so many benefits to it. When you are looking at real estate as an investment option, you are looking at it compared to the stock market, okay? Let's talk about that and break it down to basics.

Real estate versus the stock market: real estate is a tangible investment, so it will never be a zeroed asset; even if it burns down to the ground or a tornado takes it off the ground, you still have the land value.

Next, you also have what on every property? Insurance. Everything is insured, so if you are insuring it in a self-directed account and something happens, the insurance money goes back to that tax-sheltered account. If we are talking about rental properties, you have consistent, predictable income. These features help manage your risk and preserve your capital because it's a hard asset; it also produces that beautiful "A" word over time. It appreciates.

Moneeka: I love that! The beautiful "A" word!

Amanda: It appreciates over time and it cash flows simultaneously. I am not Merriam-Webster, but if you looked in the dictionary, I am pretty sure you are going to find "consistent, predictable investment income" within the definition of financial freedom. That is exactly why real estate is such a huge diversification component. Take Warren Buffett, for example. He has a huge real estate portfolio and has been noted on several occasions encouraging self-directed Roth IRAs. Do you think that is by happenstance?

Moneeka: That's a really interesting thing. People think that Warren Buffett is all about stock, or Bill Gates is all about Microsoft software. But every single person who becomes wealthy has a huge portion of their wealth in real estate or, in fact, all of it. Real estate is that common denominator with all of the wealthy, right?

Amanda: You see it all around you. Warren Buffett said on CNBC in 2012 that he would buy up "a couple hundred thousand" single-family homes if it were practical to do so, and I am sure he has some in a Roth IRA.

Moneeka: The wealthy "have it made" because they know things the rest of us kind of just don't know.

Amanda: They abide by the same rules and tax code we do. It comes down to educating ourselves. That's why I'm out here sharing some of the ninja tips on self-directed IRAs to show you that these aren't tips just for the wealthy. These are vehicles that are available to everyone.

Before I get into real estate as an investment, I want to talk about the different tax environments because that is something that not everyone fully understands. Before I get to the meat and potatoes of how real estate is so sexy and fun, I want to make sure you fully grasp the benefits of a tax-sheltered account and why you need to know the difference between your tax environments.

Does Uncle Sam always get a piece of your pie?

Moneeka: Yes, pretty much.

Amanda: Yes, he does. Now, you have been taught your whole life how to earn your income, correct?

Moneeka: Yes.

Amanda: Okay. Now the second part of that equation is how do you keep it? How do we figure out how to pay ourselves more and minimize Uncle Sam's share? I am a true-blooded American, all for everybody paying their taxes. But I'm not a fan of overpaying. I am willing to overpay to a charity as my giving back but not to the taxman.

Moneeka: Got it.

Amanda: There is a big difference when Uncle Sam gets a piece of your pie that YOU can control. When you hear "tax-deferred," think of traditional IRAs: 401(k), SEP, SIMPLE. These are all tax-deferred accounts. I told you I'm not a fan of jargon, so this means any money that you put into these types of accounts today, you get to reduce your taxable income by today; that is the instant gratification of it. The write-off. Because Uncle Sam is giving us the write-off now, guess what? He gets a piece of our pie when we turn 59 and a half and we take that money out. He gets whatever tax bracket percentage you are in at that point.

Moneeka: I just want to put in an aside here: The reason that people love this is because they make the assumption that they are going to be making less money when they start taking the money out, right?

Amanda: Hmm-mm.

Moneeka: Someone might say, I'm 40 and I'm at the height of my earning potential; my tax bracket is significantly higher today than it will be when I retire and I'm taking out this money. But I disagree. Personally, I will just say I don't plan on having a big drop in my income when I retire.

Amanda: Amen, sister.

Moneeka: Right! Those are just some things to think about and why tax-deferred may not always be the best route.

Amanda: I would call this a design flaw. This was designed back in the early 80s to help larger companies that were paying out too much in pension funds. What you just said, Moneeka, is the problem. That's what's broken in the whole philosophy that we were all spoon-fed. We were all told that you are going to be in a low tax bracket when you retire. I personally don't plan on being in a low tax bracket either. Is that the end goal for all of you successful women out there? NO, that is not part of the plan.

Let me ask you this, are taxes going up or down?

Moneeka: Up.

Amanda: Going up; so why would you put all of your eggs in the tax-deferred basket? Do you see why that's broken?

Remember the kicker: at age 70 and a half, Uncle Sam's going to come and say, "I know you want all of this nest egg to go to your kids, but too bad, so sad, you need to start paying me my cut."

Moneeka: Really?

Amanda: Yes. At age 70 and a half, the IRS makes you take money out of your IRAs [except Roth IRAs; this is why you need a CPA!]. It's called a required minimum distribution, or RMD. It's based on the cost of living and life expectancy.

Moneeka: Okay.

Amanda: Here comes 1997; who didn't love the 90s? I know I did.

Moneeka: I did, too.

Amanda: I will tell you one of the best things that came out of the 90s was the Roth IRA. Now I am going to flip this around: the opposite of a tax-deferred account is a tax-free account. Who wants to be tax free? The money that you contribute into a Roth IRA is money that you have already paid taxes on.

For example, when you get your paycheck you put money into a savings account. This is after tax. I'm sure my 90s gals remember the Friends episode with Rachel asking, "Who is FICA and why is he taking all of my money?" My point is, it's already had the taxes taken out, so Uncle Sam gets his piece of the pie on the front end. Now, instead of putting it in a savings account, put it into a Roth IRA, and here is why.

As you grow that account year after year, it's growing with compounding interest, the most powerful force on the planet per Albert Einstein. After having the account for at least 5 years and turning 59 and a half years old, you are now eligible to take that money out per the IRS.

Let's say you wanted to take out all $1,000,000 at one time at age 59.5. How much do you pay in taxes? Zero, zilch, nada, nothing in taxes.

Moneeka: Because you paid on the money that went in.

Amanda: Yes. You paid on the seed and not the crop. Uncle Sam got his piece of the pie at the very beginning, so now you get to enjoy the harvest tax free. We all typically have a "why" as far as why we invest. Majority of the clients we work with are doing it for their families. Don't we all want to leave a family legacy and create generational wealth? When you leave a Roth IRA to your children's children's children, you have created tax-free early retirement for them, and they can leave it to their children's children's children. All TAX FREE. They can still invest within that account and continue to make tax-free money from investments like real estate and have tax-free early retirements for themselves.

Tax free is a beautiful thing. There are many benefits to knowing the right tax environments, the right buckets to have your investments in; there's a monumental benefit to getting more into the Roth IRA and not having it all in tax-deferred accounts. The benefit of working with Specialized—someone like myself—is that we look at those options for you. It's not just taking a former employer's 401(k) and moving it into a Traditional IRA. We will have you look at a Roth IRA and a Roth Solo-401k and ask if you know the differences between those types of plans. We'll lay out the options that make the most sense for you. This is where education, experience, and knowledge is power. The number one remark we hear consistently is, "I wish I would have known this 10 years ago."

Don't be the shoulda-woulda-coulda person! That is why we are here today educating you and breaking down revenue code, jargon, and sophisticated strategies into plain old English that is actually quite fun when you look at the benefit side of it.

Moneeka: It's really interesting because I wish I looked at those options 10 years ago. I am actually having that emotional reaction right now. And the thing that I need to remind myself of is that, yes, it would have been great if I had known it 10 years ago, but thank goodness I know it today. You don't want to be 10 years from now thinking I wish I had known that 10 years ago.

Amanda: Absolutely. It is awareness and taking action. Now you know, and your excuses are being taken away from you. I am telling you what I am doing because I'm really big on accountability. Knowledge without action is useless. Do not be the person that cries a river about losing their retirement due to circumstances beyond their control because you have your life savings tied to the stock market. Lack of diversification and not taking action—that is a victim mindset. You have the information needed to take control and change that outcome now. It is a matter of taking action. I'll get off that soapbox, but that is a true-life scenario; I hear it all the time. Mindset and taking action are the keys to success.

Moneeka: Speaking of that, let's talk about what diversification is, why it's important, and how you work with that.

Amanda: Diversification is key, and you are not just looking at diversification of investment assets. It's diversification of tax strategies. It is diversification of accounts, having a multitude of accounts. One investment or investment category is not a portfolio; one account or account type is not a portfolio. You have to have a lot of moving parts. You need to know what parts are out there, what parts you are starting with, and what you are looking to achieve.

If real estate is your love, your passion, there are a million ways to invest in real estate without putting all of your eggs in one basket.

Take diversification within real estate for example. You can invest in buy-and-hold rentals with consistent, predictable cash flow. You can flip properties, you can form joint ventures, you can invest into commercial apartment syndications; some are for accredited investors, some are not.

You can own a percentage of that LLC that owns real estate. You can also do wholesaling within your retirement account; you can become private moneylender.

Maybe you know someone who is an HGTV-er or who is flipping properties, and you want to dip your toe into real estate, but you are not ready to go all in or swing a hammer. You can be the bank and be the private lender for those investors right from your self-directed account. They pay your account whatever terms that you set forth. If someone is borrowing money, it's the bank that sets the terms, correct? It's a very win-win situation and secured with a tangible asset. Pretty creative, right?

Investing is a family sport, correct? How many of you are entrepreneurs with kids? Every child under 18 can have a CESA. Could they have a Roth IRA, though? If you read closely, you remember they need earned income. How can a kid have earned income? Think creatively. As mothers, don't we love having our kids' pictures professionally done? Is it true that kids and animals market products to sell? (No, your dog or cat cannot have a Roth IRA.) As entrepreneurs, we are creating consistent marketing material, are we not? You pay for photographers, videographers, designers to create this marketing from your business accounts, correct? If you use their smiling faces in marketing material for your business, could you compensate them for it? Why would you do that? So your kids can have earned income and Roth IRAs!

We can take our "Big Mama" self-directed accounts and partner them with our "Baby's" self-directed Roth accounts to get them to grow by investing in non-traditional investments like real estate. Remember, there are only three ways to purchase property within a self-directed account. You can do it outright with one account, or you can partner accounts together. How many ways can you partner your family accounts together to create generational wealth?

The third way is leveraging. In a Roth Solo 401(k)—the best thing since sliced bread—you can actually leverage buy-and-hold properties in that account and not incur any type of tax implication for borrowing that money. Understand what I just said there: you are able to buy twice the amount of assets with your retirement account because you are able to use leverage. There are certain rules and regulations around that. This is not the appropriate place to dive into the details of UBIT and publication 598, but we cover that with you. Nevertheless, this allows you to maximize your purchasing power. Example: you can purchase two properties versus one. You accelerate the pay down on the loans until they are free and clear. Rinse and repeat. That snowballs over time, and guess what it builds up to? It builds up to a mountainous portfolio that is 100% tax-sheltered. Now what happens when you want to sell off these investment properties? Are you going to take a hit on long-term capital gains tax? Want to know a beautiful thing, Moneeka? Again, I'm not a CPA. When you sell property held in retirement account—Roth IRA, traditional, or 401(k)—that retirement account shields you from taxes. Therefore, there is no capital gains tax!

Moneeka: Wow!

Amanda: You just put 20% plus back in the deal.

Moneeka: That's right.

Amanda: That's 20% back to the profit side. Out of Uncle Sam's pocket and into yours.

Moneeka: And that's what grows.

Amanda: This is the juiciness I'm talking about, yes.

Moneeka: And it's not just the 20%, but it's the growth that happens on that 20%.

Amanda: Absolutely. You have already been cash flowing on that asset, so it just adds to your return on investment (ROI), your cap rate; however, you are analyzing your investment. There are just benefits beyond belief when it comes to self-directed diversification and real estate.

Take the HSA account. We all have medical expenses today, and it will only increase as we get older and our bodies require more medical maintenance. Think about what you spend today. Especially if you have crazy kids like ours, just pad in a couple visits to the ER every year. The HSA is the only plan out there that lets you have your cake and eat it too. You get the write-off today, so it's instant gratification, and you get the benefit for the delayed gratification, all tax free at the end of the rainbow. This account allows you to pay for medical expenses today and tomorrow. Huge, powerful stuff. These are some great ninja tips that I'm sharing here that I hope everyone can take action on.

As far as taking action, I am going to share a free gift because we believe in adding value and education to every person, family, and business we meet. It is the "Field Guide to Financial Freedom" found at **https://tinyurl. com/sdirabliss**. It is a visually appealing, condensed version of everything we covered and more. I practice what I preach, so I will make myself personally available to you and your family. Simply email aholbrook@IRASTC. com. You'll receive a direct link to my calendar; see when our times sync up, and let's have a conversation. Let's see how we can grow your family legacy or scale your business with self-directed IRAs.

Moneeka: That was amazingly generous, first of all. I have thousands and thousands of listeners that are hearing this, so get on Amanda's calendar before it books up.

Amanda: Glad to be of service. For everybody listening, I absolutely mean that, and the timing is everything. You have until the tax-filing deadline to get either a Roth IRA or an HSA set up for last year. You have until the end of the calendar year to set up the Roth Solo-401k. Let us help make that meeting with your CPA a good one.

Moneeka: That's right.

Amanda: We can help alleviate that burden.

Moneeka: Yes, that's awesome. So, get on Amanda's calendar and download that free report.

Before we sign off, I definitely want to go into our three rapid-fire questions; are you ready?

Amanda: Sure, I'm ready.

Moneeka: Tell us, Amanda, one super tip on getting started investing in real estate.

Amanda: My super ninja tip would be take action. Just take action and do it. I find that so many, women specifically, will learn about self-direction, diversifying with real estate, etc., but they have fear or some trepidation. Just do it. You learn more through experience. How do I do that? Open an account, it's that simple. How do you do real estate? Put something under contract. That's it. You will figure it out along the way. It is baptism by fire, but with the right team it is easy.

My number one ninja tip is—borrowing from Nike —"just do it." Take action and then you learn as you go and grow.

Moneeka: Nice, I love that. What is one strategy for being successful in real-estate investing?

Amanda: A strategy for being successful in investing in general is having the right butts in the right seats, your team, because you can't be everything to everyone. Especially as women, I feel that we are just hardwired as mothers, as wives, as givers, that we want to do everything and be everything for everybody, then we empty our cups. You cannot drink from an empty cup. So get the right butts in the right seats.

I know a lot of tax-related "stuff," but I'm not a CPA. So I have a kick-ass female CPA. I have a savvy attorney. I have the self-directed piece down, but guess what? I have mentors in this industry, too. I have mentors in the real estate industry that have done new construction, wholesaling, buy-and-holds, etc. I have industry experts I follow in other investment arenas. You should have all of these folks as well. It's putting the right butts in the right seats and bringing value to that table, too. Add value to them and they will add value to you. No one ever did it alone, and if they said they did, they are a big fat liar.

Moneeka: Did you just say that?

Amanda: I did.

Moneeka: That's so funny. Amanda, tell us one daily practice that you would say contributes to your own personal success.

Amanda: A daily practice that I do consistently? Time-blocking has really contributed to my personal and professional success. I think we all—and again, especially women—can do so many things, and we are such multi-taskers by nature. I am time-blocking my schedule, and it's a daily discipline to stick to it. I go as far as to time-block time with my husband, time for my kids, time for me, my friends, as well as my business and professional obligations. In addition to your personal business, it's useful for those of you who are working in the 9-to-5 corporate world. Just small amounts of time, little actions over time always lead to results in a big way. Those of us that are type A, myself included, find that doing time-blocking consistently is a lot tougher than we would expect. It's a disciplinary practice that leads to the desired result. What you focus on you find. Google and Outlook calendar really makes it easy.

Moneeka: Yes, it's interesting that Google calendar actually looks like blocks. I like the visual on that.

Amanda: Absolutely. A tip I got from a mentor was to line up your day and everything you are doing into 15-minute increments so you can really value your time. He suggested assigning a monetary value to it if that is how you structure your time. Then figure out what can be eliminated, what can be delegated, and what you absolutely need to do.

I continually try to do that time evaluation every quarter. I find it changes, as does life.

Moneeka: Especially when you're running a business.

Amanda: Absolutely, because your business changes. You get to new heights or plateaus, and in real estate, what's always changing?

Moneeka: The market.

Amanda: The market is forever changing, so you have to be adaptable, flexible, and willing to change with it. Otherwise, if that market changes and you want to stay fixed in the cement, it is going to leave you in the dust at the end of the day.

We have seen the cycle in the past 10 years and we are on the upside, so that's a good thing. Keep aware and stay adaptable.

Moneeka: Yes, that is awesome. This has been an amazing conversation. Thank you so much for sharing your time and wisdom with us.

Amanda: You're welcome. I am honored, and feel very blessed for everyone devoting their time to these little nuggets of knowledge. Hopefully this can be a very impactful piece for you, for your family, for generations to come.

Again, all of my contact information and resources are shared at **https:// tinyurl.com/sdirabliss**.

"It's your money, your future, so do it your way."
~AMANDA HOLBROOK

Investing Strategies to Build Wealth Blissfully

There are so many ways to build wealth in real estate. Here are several options to choose from, by experts who have done it themselves.

COMMON SENSE INVESTING TO MAKE YOU RICH
WITH KAREN BRISCOE

Moneeka: Today I'd like to welcome to the show our guest, Karen Briscoe!

Karen Briscoe is the creator of the transformative "5 Minute Success" concept. Her books Real Estate Success in 5 Minutes a Day: Secrets of a Top Agent Revealed and Commit to Get Leads: 66 Day Challenge® offer a combination of information and inspiration delivered through memorable stories. The daily format with takeaways to get into action propels one to achieve success at a higher level in business and life.

Moneeka: Hello there, Karen. Welcome to the show!

Karen: Thank you for having me! I find empowering women is one of my missions in life as well; I even have the "We Can Do It!" poster on my office wall. I was thrilled when you asked me to be on your podcast.

Moneeka: I just have to say, Karen, that it is so seductive to talk about having success in five minutes a day. How can you resist that topic, and what amazing brilliance to come up with that. How did you do that? How did the concept start?

Karen: I was working predominately with women on coaching and training to help them achieve at a higher level. Many times they said they didn't have enough time because they had many other commitments in addition to their work, and they wanted to be investing as well. The idea that they didn't have enough time resonated with me.

At the same time, women wanted to do something empowering for their life. I find personal and business development to be—for myself and for others that have achieved at a high level—one of the key aspects to going to the next level, to break through. I suggested that they should be reading and listening to podcasts, along with other personal development strategies, to help them achieve what they wanted to achieve. But over and over again, women would say they didn't have enough time. I finally asked do you have five minutes a day? And everybody said they had five minutes a day. So the idea is to make the commitment, and it really is a commitment, and an investment in yourself, to do something every day that will help you take your business and life to the next level. If you do it every day, it really becomes a habit.

There is lots of research on habit formation; the idea is if you establish the habit, then you don't have to rely on willpower. Instead you can rely on the habit. In writing Real Estate Success in Five Minutes a Day—and now speaking, coaching, and the podcast 5 Minute Success—I discovered something that is even more powerful than I thought it was when I first came up with the idea. When you think on something, particularly if you do it early in the day, it has a chance to germinate in your mind. You will find ways to put it into action or you will find ways to implement it into your business and life. That is how people have achieved success at a higher level by implementing this practice. That is where the idea came from. It is a combination of inspiration and information—that is what makes it transformative. Information alone sometimes can be very dry and boring, textbook like, and inspiration alone can be a little fluffy . . .

It is the combination of inspiration and information that becomes transformative. I say it is like peanut butter and chocolate; I mean, who doesn't love a Reese's Peanut Butter Cup? It is bringing them together that is more impactful for people to achieve at a higher level, having both.

Moneeka: You said a lot of really amazing things there, and one of my favorites is "it's a habit." I wrote the book Choose Bliss, and bliss is a choice and making that choice is a habit. The whole book is about creating habits that, over time, allow you to be in the habit of being in a good mood all the time. Honestly our mood, our ways that we react to things, the way that we live our life, those are all habits. We don't think of them as habits, but they are. We have our emotional habits, we have our mental habits, and we have our physical habits. So I just love that you called it a habit because it really is.

Something else you said that I thought was awesome is that personal development is really a huge key to success. I like to say that success is not for the faint of the heart. Because it takes a lot of internal growth in order to have the things in the world that you want and to reach the kind of success that you want. You need to be really solid in yourself and keep growing because the world, the landscape of the places where we are trying to be successful, is constantly changing.

Karen: Absolutely, that is the truth.

Moneeka: If we are not able to evolve, if we are not able to change, if we can't continue to grow with the world, then success will leave us behind.

Karen: I like the analogy that when you throw a pebble into a pond there is a ripple effect. Be the pebble; be the one that is causing the ripples because then you will have so much more impact! I have seen that women sometimes believe it is being selfish to take the time for their own personal and business development. However, if you look at the big picture and the long-term effect of when women do invest in themselves, you see that the lives of the people around them are improving, which makes it a really good investment.

Moneeka: You know that a very strong woman brings up a very strong family: our children are stronger, our communities are stronger, our husbands or our spouses are stronger. Women really are the pillar of the family. No matter what anybody says, a woman's emotional, mental, and physical strengths will impact everybody around her.

Then think about the ripple effect in real estate; there is no place that a woman can make more difference than with a home. I hope that it is okay that I am generalizing this way—because I am not saying that this is the only place where we have impact—but we understand nesting, we understand homes, we understand families. It is intuitive. And when it comes to real estate, talk about a ripple effect! You create a beautiful space, you have a family move in, that family's entire world is changed and is impacted, and that neighborhood is impacted and that community is impacted. Real estate is a huge way to create an impact in the world, one house, one family at a time, wouldn't you agree?

Karen: Yes, it is like the pebble; you can have that kind of an effect re-verberate out.

Moneeka: Awesome! Tell us about your concept of "Connect to Build and Grow."

Karen: What happens with investors, entrepreneurs, or business owners is that they will get a deal and get it through the process, then they wake up and realize that they need to get another deal. It becomes like a hamster wheel because they are just continuously only doing the next thing that takes them to the next deal. And that is not a bad way to start because everybody has to start with their first deal. But the idea of "Connect to Build and Grow" is to do the activities, then plan and put in systems to create leverage and to create an ongoing sustainable enterprise. Because that is where you will have true freedom. If you are only as good as your next deal, then as soon as you stop doing deals, you won't have anything to sustain you. It was a real epiphany in my investing life when I came to the realization that to earn money as a real estate agent—or just about any profession—you have to keep going. For instance, when a dentist stops doing dentistry, then there is no more money coming in. A dentist is only as good as the next patient. As an agent, I am only as good as the next house I sell. I realized that what I really wanted to achieve in terms of being able to live the life I wanted to live was to have a passive stream of income.

And this is where a real light bulb went on: if you want to earn $1,000,000, which is a lot of money, you really have to earn $1,300,000 to $1,500,000, because you pay taxes. You are really working way more than you want to in order to earn $1,000,000. If you had a similar investment in the stock market and you received $5,000 a month in income, you have, in effect, a $1,000,000 asset. **The objective is to get the income stream, not necessarily to get the full asset.**

The beauty of investing in real estate is that, in most cases, when people purchase their first home, they become what I call accidental investors. They own a house, a condo, or a townhouse, and then they go on to buy a new home, and keep the first property as an investment. That is probably the most typical way people become investors.

Moneeka: That is certainly the easiest way.

Karen: It is easiest, because your best financing with the least amount of money you need to put down upfront is with an owner-occupied property. On the other hand, my husband and I became accidental investors because our son moved back home after college and he couldn't find anyplace else to live—and we didn't want him living with us! So we bought a rental property and he was our first tenant. That is another way people become real estate investors.

Moneeka: Let's stop here for just a moment. I really want to highlight what Karen just mentioned because this is important. There are many, many opportunities for us to buy houses that we don't take advantage of. Karen could have decided to rent an apartment for her son until he could afford to rent his own. I have seen a similar things happen: in this case a parent wants or needs to move close to a child, and the child will rent the apartment or house next door instead of buying the apartment or house next door.

But in this particular case, Karen bought a place; she put her son in it so he was her first tenant. She got to know the place, she was not worried about her first tenants, she was not learning about the property with tenants she didn't know. By the time her son moved out, the property had appreciated, she was cash flowing, and it all happened seamlessly. She didn't buy something to spoil her son because it is an asset for her and grows her business. This is something to think about when a child is going to college and they don't want to live on campus.

Karen: Exactly, that is a brilliant strategy.

Moneeka: Maybe the first year your child wants to stay in the dorm, but then they want their own place. Your child may have friends who want to live in a house and will share the rent. So you buy a house or townhouse and it becomes an investment for you, the parents, and you can take advantage of the appreciation while your child is living there. Rents go up, so by the time your child moves out you would be cash flowing that property. If you start to tweak your thinking a little bit, as your life changes, you can think of easy ways to make real estate a piece of the growth. I just wanted to point that out because what you did was so brilliant.

Karen: I also know when elderly parents need to move closer but they are not ready to go into assisted living, this an opportunity to purchase a house. There is a whole new demographic that is opening up with the baby boomer generation aging and their parents aging. You could buy into something that is more likely to appreciate because there are more and more people that are going to need housing suited for seniors. The idea is to purchase property for 20% to 25% down, and then you own 100% of that asset. You can't go do that in the stock market!

Moneeka: Or anywhere else!

Karen: You can't buy 100% of the stock with 20% down. Another epiphany is when I realized that the tenants are paying the mortgage and I am getting 100% of an asset while building this passive income. There will be a trajectory of passive income that will eventually replace the active income that I am now earning.

Moneeka: It is about building systems, that is where we started.

Karen: Connect to Build and Grow!

Moneeka: At first, you were only buying and selling real estate for your clients.

Karen: Yes, as an agent but not for myself. I don't know why it took me so long for that light bulb to go on.

Moneeka: Then you moved within the industry in a way that you could start creating a passive income and assets so you could grow for the future. This is a really interesting topic for us to talk about because a lot of my listeners have high-paying executive W2 jobs, and they are very busy; there is a lot going on, and there are people breathing down their neck. But that doesn't mean they can't build for their future. Just like what you were saying, Karen; you were an agent, but it became important to start leveraging real estate to grow for your future, to create passive income so that you can then live your lifestyle when you retire. Many people are in that space, that situation. There are a lot of people that believe that as long as they are in W2 job, they are not going to be able to invest in real estate because it takes too much time, it takes too much effort.

Karen: Actually, you are better off because you are more likely to get financing. People who are self-employed and get W9 income have much more scrutiny in terms of getting a loan. So the W2 employee has a better financing capability than somebody who is self-employed.

Moneeka: And you can take a loan against your home equity.

Karen: You can use your home equity line of credit or IRA; there are lots of vehicles now. Talk to a lender first because you want to make sure you do it the right way. Sometimes they don't want you to take a loan to use as a down payment. When we purchase property, we use other resources to pay the down payment and then we pull the cash out of the home equity to pay back those resources. By scheduling to purchase one property every two years, we have been able to purchase four properties. One of the benefits to that strategy is when you are looking at the lending environment on buying investor properties, the lender wants to see a couple years of history, including a rental history. Then they will not claim that "debt" against your credit worthiness. We are building up this credit worthiness by being able to manage tenants, and that gives us more and more bandwidth to be able to purchase additional properties.

Moneeka: And it is streamlined and simple. This is the other point that I want to make for W2 employees: you think you don't have the time, but you can if you set up the systems like what Karen is talking about. If you set up the systems, it can take care of itself and you don't have to spend a lot of time and energy maintaining those properties. You just keep doing what you are doing and then you take advantage of both.

Karen: I think that there are a couple of key attributes to good real estate investing: one is location, location, location. If you buy in a desirable location, it almost doesn't matter what you buy because the location will raise the quality of the product up, and you will always have people who want to rent there. And you really want to go for the quality tenant. I will take less rent for a quality tenant. I want somebody who has good credit score and a good job who is not likely to be a problem tenant down the road. My husband and I have chosen to be the type of landlords that everybody wants, in terms of we are very proactive on maintaining systems, and every time a property turns over, we invest back in it because we want to take care of our asset. I know there are some situations where tenants can be challenging, but we haven't had that happen. I have helped a lot of other clients work with tenants, and those are the characteristics in quality tenants that I have seen over and over again. If you buy well in good locations and really focus on the quality tenant—with a quality job and a good credit score—then, in most cases, the tenant usually works well. You have to prepare for the possibility that someone becomes a challenge, but those are the key factors that I have always seen.

Moneeka: I run my business in a similar way. It is all about location, then I will wait for the right tenant who I do all my research on. I usually won't take lower rent, but I will wait longer to get a really good tenant because your tenant is going to be the biggest factor in whether your business is blissful or not.

Karen: Absolutely. I haven't personally had any bad tenants but I have clients that have bad tenants, and I have felt their pain. I have seen the attributes of challenging tenants and usually they have some sort of credit problems. I am not saying that they can't improve their credit score, but at the same time, poor credit is a negative indicator.

Moneeka: I agree. I am also proactive whenever there is a turnover. I want to make sure the property is beautiful so it attracts the right tenant. And because it is my asset, I want to make sure that it is being kept up, so when I finally decide to sell, it will be in good condition. And the more that you defer maintenance . . .

Karen: Oh, that just costs more in the long run.

Moneeka: Well, it costs more in the long run because then you are attracting tenants that are okay with deferred maintenance and they can tend to be a little bit more of a headache. It's all very circular! It's nice to know that we run our businesses in a similar manner.

Karen: These are some of the principles or foundational elements of the real estate investing business. Something I find interesting is that you said you would rather wait for a tenant. I am the other way around: I would rather get a tenant in there so I don't lose money. For example, let's say the rental income is $2,500 a month; if I miss one month of income, I have lost $2,500. However, if I lower the rent a $100 a month to get a tenant quicker, then even over one year, I have only lost $1,200. I could then have a rent bump the next year so I get it back up again. I find that renting is just like anything, the market responds to the changes, even a small adjustment. Sometimes I'll reduce the rent by $25 or $50 until I can find the sweet spot that triggers the activity of good quality tenants.

Moneeka: What I normally do is I go on to Zillow and Craigslist to set my price. I will take the low price and the high price, so I have a range, then I usually set mine right in the middle, even though I have a very high-quality property. I have found that when I lower my price tenants tend to nickel-and-dime me the entire time that they are in the place; they want me to pay for the light bulbs, they want me to pay for the plumber. But when someone understands about getting a good deal for a good property, that they are paying a mid-range rent on a high-range property then they are very appreciative. Those tenants will take care of all of those expenses so I don't to have the conversation every time something goes wrong. That may just be in my market, but that is why I am willing to wait. I will say, I never have a property that is vacant for more than two or three weeks.

Karen: That is pretty fast.

It is just certain times of the year in our market area when there is a lull. For example, we bought our last investment property around Thanksgiving, and I didn't want the house to be vacant through the winter. We had a good quality tenant come along—they were a young couple who just got married—and they asked for a little bit of a rent reduction. I was willing to do the reduction to get somebody in the house and we agreed to do a rent bump after 12 months.

Moneeka: You work with them.

Karen: The market is constantly changing. And you have to adjust for the market. If the market is adjusting then you have to be mindful. Right now, the market is going up rapidly, but sometimes it goes the other way, too.

Moneeka: What this conversation really proves is that there are so many good ways to do real estate. There are many ways to do it right, so just find your groove and go with that. And I just love what you said, Karen: know the things that will really make the difference, including your location and the kind of people you want to do business with as tenants and service providers. What are the ways you will research both the location and the tenants? What is the system you will put into place? What will you be most comfortable with? If I'm comfortable with something but you're not, then you don't do it my way. Or maybe you can't afford a high-end property but you want to get started; I did that, too. I started with a property that I wouldn't normally buy but I wanted to get started. This is about finding your own personal sweet spot! I love this conversation with Karen because we have seemingly the exact same strategy but we have a very different take on how we are going to implement that strategy. And this is also one of the really good reasons for hanging out with other people who are doing the same type of investing.

Karen: You will learn so much!

Moneeka: Right! Because there is wisdom in each of our lives, Karen.

Karen: Another key principle I have found is that you should be within 30 minutes of your real estate. Especially for accidental landlords, being further away is more challenging. You should be able to see the real estate within a reasonable period of time. Plus, you will be able to build a portfolio if you have some proximity. I am not saying you need to have all of the property in the same exact market; we selected different market areas for different reasons. One is near a metro station, another because of the schools, another because of new growth and jobs. We were looking at different factors when we choose the locations, and they are all within about 30 minutes drive from us. Particularly in the beginning, I would recommend people follow this guideline.

Moneeka: I started with within 30 minutes and have grown to within an hour.

Karen: Wow! In California you sometimes have to go a distance to be able to afford real estate.

Moneeka: That is right, especially to be able to get into a specific market. Everybody is not able to do what I do, and that's okay. It's a guideline. It doesn't mean this is the only way to do real estate—it is the way that I have chosen—but you can still take the principles that Karen and I are talking about and implement them. You just need to find your sweet spot. That is the key.

Karen: I love how you keep using "sweet spot," and we are going to talk about that.

Moneeka: Yes, let's talk about the sweet spot of success!

Karen: Another aspect we should talk about is to commit to get leads. This is going and finding the property. That is your lead generation. The process is you buy it, get it ready to rent, get your tenant. The "Connect to Build and Grow" is creating systems and leverage so it is ongoing and sustainable, and then success thinking, success activities, and success vision. Moneeka has talked about mindset and motivation to keep your bliss. You are choosing bliss and you are keeping it through this whole process, and when that all comes together is when you get to your sweet spot.

You will be balancing or adjusting, so sometimes you may focus more on finding properties, finding deals. Sometimes you may be deep in the weeds of the process. Sometimes you are looking at the larger vision and creating your plan or putting in the systems to leverage. And the whole time—it is completely encompassing—you are being mindful of your habits, your motivation, and your mindset. As you do this, you get to your sweet spot.

Moneeka: I love that! It's really creating an infrastructure or ecosystem for success.

Karen: Yes, that is a great analogy. It is an ecosystem because it is constantly adjusting and adapting for the market and for your situation. You may have to readjust some of your focus at different times but, at the same time, you keep in mind what you are trying to achieve.

Moneeka: Awesome! I feel like we can just keep talking and talking, but we are out of time.

Karen: I am glad that we were able to visit.

Moneeka: Karen, can you tell my audience how they can get in touch with you.

Karen: There are several ways: the website is 5minutesuccess.com, on Facebook there is a group with lot of tips and strategies, and there is the 5 Minute Success podcast where I interview entrepreneurs, coaches, and sales professionals—many of them talking about real estate.

Moneeka: Awesome! I know that you are offering my audience a very generous gift; could you tell us about that?

Karen: I am offering a seven-day quick start, which is a daily reader, to get you into the groove of setting up habits. As we talked about, it is habits that help propel you to achieving at a higher level, and this seven-day quick start will get you going.

Moneeka: Perfect! Karen, are you ready for our three rapid-fire questions?

Karen: Absolutely.

Moneeka: First, tell us a super tip on getting started investing in real estate.

Karen: I want to share this proverb: "When is the best time to plant a tree? It was 20 years ago. The next best time is now." So the best time to buy real estate was 20 years ago, but the next best time is now! People may think that they missed the market, that they should have bought in 2009 when the market was down. But I say that if you buy well and you stay in for the long term—this is a long-term vision—then you will be glad in 20 years that you bought now.

Moneeka: I would like to add to that. When I was taping a television segment a couple of months ago, I was speaking to the producer of the program. He wanted to talk about real estate and said, "You know, the market is just too high; I wish I had bought 10 years ago." And I said, "Yes, and you are going to be saying that exact same thing in 10 years, so buy now!" Such good advice, Karen, thank you.

Tell us one strategy on being successful in real estate investing.

Karen: We have talked about a couple of the strategies, but here is one that I have seen to be the most successful. If you buy an owner-occupied property and you plan to buy a new property in a couple years, don't over-buy. Don't use all of your capability to buy the first property; buy a new property in a couple of years and keep the first property. I have found that this generates wealth for people faster than any other method. And don't forget the other alternatives that we talked about: look for family members or friends who you can invest in real estate for them or with them and build your portfolio that way.

Moneeka: Nice, thank you. Finally, Karen, could you tell us one daily practice that you would say contributes to your own personal success?

Karen: There is a quote I really like: "People do not decide their futures, they decide their habits, and their habits decide their futures." Habits are dependable, they will sustain you whether or not you are inspired, or whether you feel like it or not, or whether you feel persistent or not. If you start creating good habits, then you will achieve a higher level of success in both your business and your life.

Moneeka: I love that, thank you so much. This has been such a great show! Thank you for all of that wisdom and all of those little bits of information that we can take out into our lives.

> *"Ultimately, there's one investment that*
> *supersedes all others: Invest in yourself."*
> ~WARREN BUFFETT

PASSIVE INCOME MADE EASY
WITH OUT-OF-STATE RENTALS
WITH MAUREEN MCCANN

Moneeka: Today, I'd like to welcome to our show our guest, Maureen McCann. Maureen, co-founder and principal owner of Spartan Invest, operates as the VP of sales and marketing for the boutique real estate investment company. Spartan Invest is recognized as one of the top two real estate investment companies in the US that specializes in providing investors turnkey real estate for monthly passive residual income.

Maureen brings with her ten years of sales and marketing experience in the turnkey marketplace. Having served as an investment property coach for years, Maureen is skilled in helping clients build turnkey cash flow portfolios for her clients. Maureen has helped hundreds of investors build the type of rental portfolios necessary to reach their short-term and long-term monthly passive income goals. Maureen understands true wealth is created in the mind first and the properties second. It is about setting the mind right and programming the mind to "think and grow rich." Maureen credits many books for her success, but the top two books she credits for going from a W2 wage earner to business owner and real estate investor are Think and Grow Rich by Napoleon Hill and Rich Dad, Poor Dad by Robert Kiyosaki. These books rewired her scarcity mindset and transformed her thinking into an abundance, wealth-creating mindset. Maureen is known for saying, "You can never become wealthy with a broke mindset. There is not one wealthy person walking this earth who achieved their goals with a broke mindset. Period. Change the way you think and change your life. "

Investing in turnkey real estate for long-term wealth generation is something Maureen is very passionate about. Maureen is an advocate for financial literacy and for creating wealth through real estate. Whether clients want to replace their current income with passive income, retire their J-O-B, pay for college for kids or clients are simply looking to supplement their retirement, Maureen custom designs the right portfolio with the right end goal in mind. Hello, Maureen? Welcome to the show.

Maureen: Hi, there. Oh my gosh, what a very nice long intro. But in short, here's what I do: I just help people make money. Cash flow is my middle name. If you like cashflow, let's talk, girl.

Moneeka: That's why you're on this show.

Maureen: Beautiful. I like making money and I love, I love, love, love helping other people make money. It's fun. You make a lot of friends that way.

Moneeka: Well, you make friends that way and it's so gratifying, isn't it? Like, to watch people have that success and create the blissful lives they want. So Maureen, why don't you start by just telling us your story.

Maureen: I would love to. I think my story will resonate with a lot of the investors and our #lady-bosses out there. So, my story is I'm an East Coast girl, born in Philly, raised in New Jersey. Made my trek out to San Diego 28 years ago. I basically told my family, "Hey, I am moving to San Diego, California. I am leaving in 5 days." Now, what you need to know is that I did not know one person in San Diego. As a matter of fact, I had never even been to San Diego before. I just knew, in my soul, that SD was where I was supposed to be. I felt it in my gut. There was something about the place that I was being pulled to.

So, in August 1991, with my red little Nissan Pulsar packed with all of my stuff, I boldly drove across the country by myself, at just 20 years young. You see . . . I did something. I made a radically bold decision to leave the herd. And the herd, with their "stay together" mentality, began to inadvertently reveal their fears and their reasons why they would never do such a thing through their comments like, "It is too expensive in California." "It's the land of the fruits and the flakes." "Why are you moving there?" "Oh, you'll be back."

And for a hot minute, I almost let their fears stop me from pursuing my dreams. I almost let their reasons for holding them back hold me back. Can anyone relate to this? Can anyone relate to wanting to follow their gut, follow the thing that's pulling them, to follow a dream, only to have those closest to you shut it down with their fears on why THEY wouldn't do it?

Be careful about letting other people's words occupy your thoughts. Listen to your own voice. Follow that one. The one inside of you that really tells you what your heart wants. I was resolute in my decision to go to California, and nothing or no one was going to derail me.

I made a decision that day. I chose not to follow the herd and I hit the road . . . living by my own rules. One thing I have learned is that making radically bold decisions leads to radically bold outcomes.

Moneeka: I can actually relate to that.

Maureen: You know, I have come to learn a lot of things around decision-making. I have learned that if you make a decision and it scares you a little bit, then most likely it was the right decision. Those nervous butterflies tell you that you are moving out of your comfort zone and you are stretching yourself into growth. This is a great thing! Celebrate it.

I have also come to know that our lives are a direct reflection of how we think and the decisions we make. I realized something from watching my hard-working parents sometimes work multiple jobs just to support their three kids. My strong work ethic comes from watching how hard they worked, and to them I am so grateful.

What I also learned, though, is you can work very hard and still wind up with very little in your golden years. I saw this happen to them and many others as the amount of money they had in their retirement accounts went down whenever the stock market went down. The great financial crisis of 2008-2009 left many retirement accounts battered and beaten. And with very little time left for seniors to recover their losses, they simply either had to go back to work in their mid-60s or they would have to live off less. I had decided in that moment that I did not want this to happen to me, my kids, or anyone else for that matter. I saw they had very little control over their retirement accounts when the earnings were based off of the whims of the market. I realized that day that I needed to do something different. I knew that day that I needed to find a way to get my money to earn money versus me working for it. And I needed to find a way to do it outside of Wall Street.

I had learned a very valuable lesson from my parents' choice to trade their time for money. There are only 24 hours in a day. You cannot make more time just to make more money. That is an impossibility. The only other option is to find ways to make your money make more money for you. Leveraging other people's time is a great option.

On one sunny San Diego summer day, I remember driving along the Pacific Coast Highway, and up on the hilltop were these beautiful, million-dollar homes overlooking the Pacific Ocean, and I thought, "What did the owners of those homes know that I didn't know?" They knew something different than I did, but it didn't mean that I couldn't learn it.

So, that's when I started fiercely pursuing my real estate education. I joined my first Mastermind and then a second. I hired mentors and coaches. I dove head first into learning all that I could about real estate. I had my eye on the prize. I wanted one of those houses on top of the hill. I remember kind of fantasizing about those houses on the hill, but I was a W2 wage earner. And honestly, I was very comfortable. I was in the pharmaceutical world, I was making good money. And when you're single, that's great. And then I got married, and it was still great because then we had two incomes, no kids, living a great life.

Then the first baby came, then the second baby came, and then the third baby came. And what I realized is that as the expenses increased, the pay didn't increase as fast as the expenses were increasing. And I realized that my 1 to 2% increases every year were not outpacing inflation. Financially, I realized I was not going anywhere. I was a hamster on the wheel, trading my time for money, running as fast as I could yet getting nowhere fast financially.

I remember a coach asked me, "Maureen, what's your definition of wealth?" I said . . . (actually, I didn't really know what to say, and I just kind of threw out) "Oh, it's financial freedom. I can just do whatever I want." And he's like, "Nice swing, but a miss." I laughed and said, "Okay, if you're going to tell me then, what's the definition of wealth?"

He said, "Wealth is an equation. And your return on investment must beat inflation. So, whatever it is, whether it's residential real estate, commercial real estate, oil and gas, a startup app, whatever your investment is, your rate of return must beat the inflationary rate. That's how you generate wealth." Light bulb moment.

That clicked in my mind, and I realized that in my W2 world, with my wages incrementally increasing 1%-2% every year (and with inflation around 6%), I realized I was never going to earn my way to wealth on one stream of income. Not on those types of annual raises. I realized I was going to have to invest my way to wealth by creating multiple streams of income through rental properties.

Side note: Some readers may push back on my stated 6% inflationary rate. This is certainly not a number the US Bureau of Labor Statistics publishes. Their number is much lower, but if you really want to check out some interesting data looking at Consumer Inflation-Official Vs Shadowstats, go to John William's ShadowStats.com website. You will find the analysis shows the not-seasonally-adjusted Consumer Price Index for Consumer Inflation is nearly 6%. If you just think about basic mathematics, your 1 to 2% increases every year are never going to beat out the 6% inflationary rate. You're always going to be trying to catch up, never getting ahead. Does this make sense?

Moneeka: I really, really want to highlight that point, because we all hear this, "Oh you have to keep up with inflation." What does that even mean? And you said a really interesting thing, that here you were, you were in the pharmaceutical industry, you were making really, really good money, you had a really good life. But even you didn't really understand that inflation was rising faster than your income. All you knew was, "My income wasn't meeting my needs anymore."

And I think there are a lot of women that are listening to this show that are having that same experience. And there's this sort of Twilight Zone thing. You're thinking, "What is going on that I'm not getting?" Did you have that experience?

Maureen: 100%.

Moneeka: It's so interesting because the government says these numbers, and what are they based on? For instance, if they include housing, then inflation is huge in places like California. Right?

Maureen: So true.

Moneeka: What are those numbers really all about? And we get really locked into, "The government says it's this number and so it is. So, now I've just got to make 3%." And what you've discovered is that it's not 3%. We have to make significantly more than 3% to get ahead.

Maureen: I'm going to add two points here. One is, I thoroughly agree with you—if you want to just create wealth, you have to beat inflation. So, if inflation is 6%, you got to have returns of 7, 8, 9, 10, 11%. The higher, the better because you're accelerating your dollars.

Moneeka: Right, and that's if your expenses don't increase. That's just with inflation. Right?

Maureen: That's true.

And then I think the other point your listeners could relate to, just as my own experience taught me, was we all were kind of brainwashed into thinking that your 401k is your end-all, be-all. If anyone really does history on the 401k, you're going to recognize that the 401k was a substitute for corporations for pensions, because the pension plans are way too expensive to fund. According to Robert Kiyosaki in his new book, Why the Rich Get Richer, the 401K was created to make the Wall Street cats richer, not the investor.

You and I live in California. The last report that I saw, 51% of the pensions in California are underfunded, which means they can't pay the benefits that they promised people because of how expensive those pension plans are. So, of course, we just keep getting taxed more and more and more.

So, after studying, I realized that my 401k plan was a nice substitute for a pension plan, but it wasn't my end-all, be-all. But many of your listeners may still think that "If I max my 401k and my company matches it, I'm going to be set for life." Many investors waking up decades later, after they placed their first dollar in their 401k in 1978, are finding out there is not enough money in those accounts to sustain them for the rest of their lives. Retirement is not the time to find out you do not have enough money saved to carry you through the rest of your life.

For me, I learned that you can max out your 401k contributions plus get your company to match up to 6. When the market worked in my favor and my quarterly statements were in the black, I loved this.

But then the red started showing up. And I don't just mean one quarter. I mean quarter after quarter after quarter, my 401k statements were in the red. I was consistently losing money, and yet my money manager continued to earn money even though he was losing mine. I did not like this at all.

And as I found myself staring at yet another red quarterly statement, I remember how powerless I felt. My 401k was hemorrhaging, and I didn't know how to stop it. It was then I realized I had no control over the market or my money. And I can assure you, many of your listeners heard the same thing from their financial advisors as I heard from mine, who kept saying, "This is temporary. The market will rebound and you will earn your money back. Just keep your money in the market." Not very comforting or wise words from an advisor who was still collecting his quarterly paycheck from me. I remember asking my FA why I should keep investing money in the stock market. His response was a very definitive, "for diversification." I like what Robert Kiyosaki says about diversification. He said, "Diversification is not a strategy that helps you NOT lose money."

This was when I said to myself, "Time out, something's not right," and here's where my life changed.

As a drug rep, you spend a lot of time in your car. I turned my car into a mobile university as I began to listen to audiobooks and podcasts about money. I was highly focused on developing a wealth consciousness. Like Tony Robbins says, "Where focus goes, energy flows." My focus was on learning about money. How it works. How to create it. How to make more of it.

From time to time I would turn off the audiobook and listen to the radio. One day, I am driving in my car and I hear on the radio, "Hey, come learn how to flip real estate in LA. The first 100 callers are free." The false urgency hooked me and I was speed-dialing the number because I wanted to get in for free. And my fierce competitive nature wanted to beat out the other callers. Funny thing is, their tactic worked, and not just with me but with a thousand other callers, too. I found myself among a sea of people seeking a better way since their current way of earning money was not enough. The human mind loves the word "FREE," and it worked to fill the room.

So there I am in the room, and what happened in those three days changed the course of my life. Because at the end of those three days, I had to make a decision. I had to decide if I was going to DO something different or stay the same. I remember sitting in my chair on day three, already conjuring up all of the "legitimate reasons" (aka EXCUSES) for why I couldn't do this. Why I couldn't afford this course. Why I didn't have the time to complete the work. Excuse after excuse after excuse occupying the roadways of my neural circuitry. They hadn't even made the sales pitch yet, and my mind is already telling me all of the reasons why I can't. It takes courage to ignore that negative chatter, to resist the fear that anchors us in stagnation and mediocrity.

Now came the pivotal moment in my life. I was either going to make a change that day, or I was going to make an excuse for why I can't do it. I knew enough going into this free three-day seminar that your life is really a reflection of the way you think and the decisions that you make. And I knew I was facing a very big decision. Either sign up and join this expensive real estate course or go back to my same old ways of doing things.

I can tell you with 100% certainty that had I made a different decision that day, I would not be here as a guest on your show today.

After three days of listening to these real estate gurus on how to flip properties, I had to decide if what I was hearing was true or just really great salesmanship. I needed to quickly discern if I was being conned or if this was legitimate information. I needed to decide what was true for me in that moment because I knew the sales pitch was coming, and that meant I needed to make a decision here very soon or I was going to miss out on an opportunity. That FOMO (fear of missing out) thing is for real and is a great tactic to get a human to take action.

My nervous system knew it was coming, too, since my pounding heart and sweaty palms told me so. My preoccupied mind with its vacillating thoughts of "they are conning me" to "they are telling me the truth" was in an overdrive state of flux. Thoughts were swirling, and all the while I was sitting there thinking about what was I going to do once they made the offer. I could hear it coming. The pitch was getting closer and my heart is racing faster, and it felt like my mind was getting more cluttered with banter from the two voices arguing in my mind. My negative voice saying "this is a con" and my positive voice saying "this will change your life." And then I heard it: "The total value of this program is $25,000, but if you sign up today you can get the course for a low $9,995!" It was time to make a decision. Do nothing, or do something different.

The excuses started flowing in. "I can't afford it. I don't have that kind of money. I can't do it. My spouse will never agree to this. People will think I am crazy." And I did what many others would not do. I pushed all of that self-limiting, negative chatter out of my mind and I made the decision to invest in myself. I chose to invest in my financial education. I wrote that check that day for $9,995 with a very shaky and sweaty palm. I did not even have the $10,000 readily available. I had to borrow the money from my 401k plan. The backlash that I got from family and friends about all of the compound interest I would be losing out on was palpable. I chose to ignore them and their warnings. I made the decision to sign up because I knew the wealthy had a significant portion of their financial holdings in real estate. At that point in time, I had only owned one piece of real estate, my personal residence. I knew I needed to change that, and I would rather invest $10,000 in my education versus making a $50,000 mistake in real estate. So, I ignored everyone and signed up for the course. I did the opposite of what the herd was telling me to do.

The entire course of my financial life was set in a new direction with that one decision I made back in 2005. In short, had I not made that decision to invest in my financial education that day, I would have not met my first business partner, Randy Hausauer. Randy introduced me to a Mastermind Group called Fortune Builders. Fortune Builders led me to a turnkey company out of Memphis where I purchased my first two rental properties. Memphis led me to Birmingham, where I met my present-day business partners Lindsay Davis and Clayton Mobley. We founded our first turnkey company out of Birmingham, Alabama in 2013 called Spartan Invest. In five short years, Spartan Invest is now recognized as one of THE BEST turnkey companies in the United States, winning the prestigious INC 5000 Fastest-Growing American Companies Award five consecutive years in a row.

Had I let fear deter me from making that one decision, I would not have the life I have today. I learned to walk through the fear, to face it head on. I have learned everything you want is on the other side of everything you fear. Fear is just a construct in your mind. It is not real. It is perceived as real. And if fear is just a construct in your mind that you put there, then it can be deconstructed and removed. The interesting thing about fear and excitement is that, physiologically, they show up as the same thing (heart racing, sweaty palms, shortness of breath). The only difference is how your mind perceives the situation at hand.

I remember feeling afraid of investing in my first rental property. I did it sight unseen. I had a very high degree of faith and trust in my business partner's decision-making skills. Randy had a track record of surrounding himself with successful people who, too, made good decisions. So when he suggested I purchase my first investment property, I hesitated. Not because I didn't trust him or his advice. I hesitated because of my fear of losing money. You see, I am not the early adopter. I am more of the "sit back and watch" kind of investor.

So, for all of your listeners out there, I'm not the one who says, "Yeah, that sounds great, let's jump in and do it." I'm more like, "No, you put your money in first, and then I'm going to pepper you with questions for an entire year to see if it actually works."

Moneeka: And I'm that second person, too. I'm always thinking, "I don't want to be at the bottom of the upswing. I want to be somewhere between the first quarter and the first half. I want to know that things are going to go up." So, I'm totally with you on that. There needs to be proof before I jump in.

Maureen: Exactly. So my friend, Randy, bought two properties with this Memphis-based company, and I kept checking in with him periodically. I kept asking, "Randy, you still getting those rent checks?" He kept saying, "Yup." Six months later, "Randy, still getting those rent checks?" He still said, "Yeah." Then I'm thinking, "Dang, this passive income thing works."

So, I bought two rental properties, and when they were cash flowing, that's when I learned that passive income via rental properties really works. The idea of multiple streams of income came from the reading I was doing at the time. Multiple properties means multiple streams of income. I realized I had multiple bills going out each month on just one income. I realized I wanted multiple streams of income to cover the multiple bills I had. This just made so much sense in my mind.

So, passive income was what I was going to pursue. And then I realized that I'm a "lazy" investor. I like to not do anything and still make money.

Moneeka: I don't know anybody else like that. (Kidding.) It's awesome.

Maureen: And so here's what happened next, in short.

All the physicians I was meeting in my job, they were just hungry for and wanting to know how to make money. They were eager to hear about passive income through rental properties. What many people do not realize is these MDs are extremely busy practitioners whose reimbursements have been significantly reduced over the years. They have to see more and more patients each day to be able to meet their overhead. Imagine being a doctor and your former daily case load was a manageable 15 patients a day. Today, these MDs have to see 30-40 patients a day just to make ends meet. These doctors were looking for a way out. They were looking for new ways to make money.

And when I started talking to them about passive income and rental properties, their ears perked up. And in short, this is what happened. A lot of my doctors wound up buying rental properties through me as an affiliate marketer for the company that I had purchased properties from myself. So, I put my own money in, proved that it worked. And then I started recruiting my doctors.

I brought a lot of business into this company in Memphis that they just turned around and said, "Hey, would you like to join our company?" And I thought, "I think this is my opportunity to get out of the W2 world and try this."

So, I took the leap--that was 10 years ago. And that got me into the Memphis company for about five years. And then that led me to meeting my two current business partners, and we started our own turnkey company in Birmingham. And we have had five years of incredible success.

So, here's what I'm going to say to summarize all of this. Had I not written that check, had I not believed in myself enough to take the leap, I would have not accomplished anything worthy of your invitation to contribute to this book. I know with 100% certainty had I not written that check, nothing would have changed. None of this would have happened. I wouldn't be sitting here with you, I'd still be probably in pharmaceuticals getting laid off and rehired because that's what is happening to my friends who are still in that space. No one really values them.

So, if I can impart anything, any solid message to these powerful women that are listening, is when you do the thing that scares you, the results are beyond comprehension.

Moneeka: Right, and what I really love about that story is that it wasn't that the $10,000 check was the end-all. It's not the thing that saved your life. It was a step in the right direction. It was the step that took you to the next step that took you to the next step.

I think that this is something that we as investors really need to remember, is that we always have another place to go. There's another step. There's more learning, there's more wisdom, there's more experience, but that goes both ways. There's always more and there's never enough.

So, for those of you that are listening and thinking, "I don't know enough," yeah, but neither do I. Neither does Maureen because we're constantly learning. So, you can always start from exactly where you are, but you just have to take action.

Maureen: Yes, so true. I needed to make something happen and I needed to be accountable to the $10,000 I had invested. I wanted something for my $10,000 and I was willing to work for it. I have to admit for the longest time I sat on the sidelines rolling my eyes at professional coaching. I had attended a lot of seminars and I would always hear the same "take action now" message. I believed for the longest time that the "take action, take action now" pitch was just that: a pitch. I figured it was just another tactic to separate me from my money. (And I was not going to fall for that trick! They are not going to get me!)

So, I sat on the sidelines for years not making any progress nor making any more money. I sat there with my arms folded tightly across my chest, just closed off from any coaching opportunity. I would go to these free seminars, listen for three days and then do nothing. I would not hire them. I did not ask for their help, and my progress stalled. Until one day, I did. I let them "trick" me into taking action, and thank God they did because my life has been better ever since. So, I learned the value of asking for help. The day I hired my first coach was the day my professional life changed forever. I am sure many of your readers are just like me. They are the "I can do it myself" personality type. Great outcomes are the result of great people working together, not individually, to create great results. Once I understood asking for help was not a weakness but an actual strength, then my whole life started to change. And let me tell you something, once I wrote the check and dove in, I have since hired many coaches and joined many Masterminds. I am in three Masterminds currently that I pay hefty fees to be in every year because I'm surrounding myself with people that I'm learning from who are successful.

It doesn't even necessarily have to be in real estate, but they're successful in their field. Whether it's digital marketing, commercial real estate, advertising. You're in a room with these people from whom you're finding out what it is that's working for them and think, "I'm going to take that, implement that into my business and then measure the results."

I wouldn't be getting that if I was tuning into cable, which I don't have. I don't do any of that stuff. I don't have shows that I watch. I read books, I go to Masterminds, I'm a total nerd. I love to network with people and pick their brain. I network, thinking "I want to just get all the good stuff out of your brain. I'm going to share with you all the good stuff in my brain to see if we can elevate each other."

Moneeka: I love that. Because I'm the same way. I haven't watched television in 25 years. I'm exactly like you, a total nerd. I read books. I like go to Masterminds. And one of the things that I've learned from that, too, is that picking a mentor, picking a class, picking a Mastermind, is in its own right a skill. Because you do really need to find those places that are really going to further your business.

I've paid thousands and thousands of dollars for Masterminds where I got nothing or classes that I got nothing. But if I had given up and not just honed my skills, I wouldn't be where I am today. Instead I thought, "Okay, that didn't work, I need to hone my skills better to figure out what is going to work for me." So instead of, "Oh shoot, I spent all that money, what a dork, I should have known better," it's, "What can I learn from that experience?" and "Don't give up on myself, and don't give up on this idea of the Mastermind." Which if you've ever read Think and Grow Rich, you know that's one of the skills of the very, very rich.

I love also that you were saying that you often thought, "They're not going to get me." But eventually, you'd gotten to a point where you had been to enough of these intros that you had an idea of what you might be looking for, and what the differences are. That's valuable too.

I also tell people, the very first three-hour or three-day session that you go to, don't spend $30,000.

Maureen: Yes, great advice. Excellent advice.

Moneeka: Check out some of the different companies, don't get all swept up in the energy of the room.

Maureen and I are not saying go out and take the very first mentor or the very first class that you see, but we are saying take action towards your progress.

Maureen: Without a doubt. It's one step and then the next step. There was one Oprah Super Soul Sunday segment that I watched once, and she just said when she was starting her network—she started the OWN Network. She said when you take action, you just take one step. And then the next question is, "What's the next best step?" Then you take that. And then after that, you go, "What's the next best step after that?"

Moneeka: I love that. Maureen, I'd like to move onto the topic of leverage because it's so important in real estate. Let's talk specifically about how to use leverage in your business, turnkey investing.

Maureen: Okay, so I love real estate. I love real estate, I love leveraging other people's time, other people's money. And when you do it well, you can build wealth in an accelerated fashion.

Turnkey investing is about building wealth slowly over time through real estate. It is about putting a plan in place and executing the plan. It's really kind of simple.

With leveraging, I get investors to think about it this way: think big picture. In your investor's minds, if I could paint the idea of owning 10 rental properties . . . This is not 10 California rental properties, people. This is out-of-state, in markets where your price points are between $80,000 and say $120,000. So, let's just go with a $100,000 property.

If you had 10 of them (and 10 times 100,000 equals a million), you don't need $1 million to acquire $1 million worth of real estate. This is the beautiful thing about leverage. You only need a certain percent of that. Usually 20% if you're going with conventional financing. So, $200,000 would buy you $1 million and you would control $1 million worth of real estate.

Now, here's where other people's time and other people's money comes into play. I love that the banks will finance 80% of your investment. There is no bank financing for your stocks. If you want to buy Google stock at $400 a share, no one is going to give you the money for 80% of your stock purchase. You have to come up with that full amount yourself.

In real estate, the banks will lend 80% of your purchase (and take 80% of the risk). So, to get to the million dollars of real estate, do you need to buy it all today? No. What if you invested in one property a year for the next 10 years? That's a $20,000 investment each year. If that's too much of a stretch, what if you do one every two years? Whatever your acquisition period is, it's customizable to you, your needs, your goals, your timeline.

But I want you guys to think big picture because if you want to be a millionaire, no one's going to just hand it to you. You have to earn it. You have to think your way to it. And real estate is the fastest way and best vehicle I have learned that helps investors get there. I can tell you after working as a W2 wage earner for 15 years, I never became a millionaire working for someone else. I've been in real estate for 10 years, and I hit that goal halfway through. So, if you want this to happen for you, you just have to try it. And here's how you do it.

You use $20,000 of your own capital to acquire a property, an asset worth $100,000. You know what you just bought? You think you bought a house, but you really just bought a revenue stream. You bought a revenue stream of, on average, about $4,000. In my market in Birmingham, $20,000 will net you $4,000 annually. So when you look at your return on equity (ROE), here is the simple formula:

Profit divided by equity—you can clearly see a ROE of 20%!

That's 20% return on your money every year. Now, wait a minute, hold on, that's just on the cash flow. That's not on the appreciation. You only capture that on the exit, but it's still a part of your profit and it's a great hedge against inflation. You get depreciation every single year for 27.5 years, so that reduces your tax liability through that depreciation table.

So, between the cash flow, the loan paydown, the depreciation, the appreciation, plus the hedge against inflation, you are earning in multiple ways. And what I like to get investors to think about is, let's say you took 10 years. What if you took 20 years to build a portfolio of 10 rental properties? That's a total of $200,000 in investment capital that now controls $1 million worth of real estate. With us, the monthly rent on a $100,000 property is $1,000 a month. The cash flow on that is about $300 bucks. All expenses are paid, you're done, your net is $300.

If you have 10 properties at 300, that's $3000 coming in passively, mailbox money. This is your money working for you. And guess who's paying your mortgage? The tenants. Oh, I forgot, guess who's reducing your principal every year on that property?

Moneeka: Your tenants.

Maureen: Exactly! When you finally get all of the debt paid off, you will have a steady stream of thousands of dollars in cash flow each month. Many investors think it is going to take a very long time to pay off the debt. They enter the loan with a 30-year fixed rate, but that does not mean it is going to take you 30 years to pay off the loan. It's not going to take you 30 years to pay off an $80,000 note, especially if you've got 4, 5, 10 rental properties that are cash flowing. You simply aggregate the cash flow and you pay off the debt on one property at a time, and it's an accelerated payoff.

So, to give your readers an example, because I've done the calculations a thousand times, it's this; if you had 10 rental properties and you had $3,000 coming in per month, and your mortgage payment on an $80,000 note at 6% right now is around $476. So if your monthly is $476 and you are paying $3,000 towards that $476 each month, then that property is paid off in two years and a month. Just do the math. Math is money and money is fun. Just give it a try and run the numbers through a mortgage calculator with extra payments. The results will surprise and delight you. Thank the banker for lending you the money and then quickly pay off the note, save yourself thousands in interest, and have the tenant pay off your asset for you. It is a brilliant strategy.

And once your tenant has paid off your $100,000 asset, you now have a line of credit available to you which you can draw on any time. This is the source of capital you can mobilize to lever into additional cash flowing assets like real estate. In addition, you have a property with monthly rent of $1000. Remember, you still have to pay taxes, insurance, and property management fees. After you deduct these expenses, your rental property will produce anywhere from $750-$800 a month. That equates to $9600 a year in monthly passive residual income. Imagine multiplying this number by the number of properties you own. This is where owning multiple rental properties becomes very interesting.

Imagine owning 10 rental properties with each one of them producing $9600 a year. 10 properties multiplied by $9,600 a door per year produces an annual income of $96,000 per year. $96,000 of residual income is a very nice retirement plan. Investing in turnkey rental properties is just one type of investment strategy. It is an excellent way to help provide you and your family monthly passive residual income. The idea simply is to invest a little bit of your money and leverage a lot of someone else's money and put it into a property, and then let other people's time and money (the renter) work to pay down your debt, increase your equity position, give you the monthly cash flow, while taking advantage of the annual depreciation you can take on your tax schedule every year for the next 27.5 years. Then one day you're going to wake up 10 years from now owning a million-dollar rental portfolio and guess what? Ed McMahon is not going to knock on your door and congratulate you on becoming a millionaire. It will just happen silently over time. The day will arrive where all of your rentals are paid off and your million dollars' worth of real estate will yield you a large annual income.

And all of this happened because you . . .

Moneeka: Planned for it.

Maureen: Planned for it and executed it really well.

The best way to acquire rental properties is to lever into them. Just use a little bit of your money and a lot of a bank's money to acquire these properties.

Moneeka: I had a specific question about that strategy. So, here in California, once you get five loans, it's hard to get the next loan. So you're talking about getting 10 loans. Talk to me a little bit more about that detail.

Maureen: Absolutely! We as investors are allotted 10 Golden Tickets. Fannie Mae will allow investors to carry 10 individual mortgages. This means we have 10 Golden Tickets that allow us to get into 10 loans. Some lenders will only lend up to four loans before requiring you to find another bank to qualify you for the remaining six loans. This can be an inconvenience to the investor/borrower. I have lenders whom I have come to know and trust who will do up to 10 individual loans.

It is important to keep in mind that it is a rolling 10. So, if you had 10 mortgages, as one's paid off, now you have an open slot and you can go get another one.

So, what you ideally want as a real estate investor is to find one lender who can do all 10 for you. Because they've got all your paperwork and it makes it convenient and easy for you. I do have lenders. After 10 years of being in the business, I've identified the lenders that can do 10 and won't kick you out after four or five.

Moneeka: Wow! Okay, awesome. The rates are just a little higher, I'm guessing?

Maureen: It's the same, really. And here's the other thing that's interesting, is that in lending, I've seen products show up and then they disappear, and then they cycle back in and then they show up again. Like the portfolio loans, they're back.

For your listeners that don't know, a portfolio loan is you can group multiple properties under one loan, and it will show up on your credit report just as one loan. But you could have four or five or six properties under that loan. And you can do it either way. You can buy a bunch of properties individually, refinance under a portfolio loan. Now, that's a little bit of a higher interest rate. It's more work for that lender to do that.

Or the other way is get pre-qualified for a portfolio loan and then go out and buy four or five (or however many you want) properties. And it will show up as one. I have investors that want 50 properties. So, there's got to be a way to be able to utilize the conventional financing of just a small percentage down, but not use up all their 10 Fannie Mae slots. This is one way to do it.

Moneeka: Interesting, I love that. Maureen, how can my audience reach you? And I know you've got a free gift for everybody, so tell them a little bit about that.

Maureen: Yes. So, all of you beautiful powerhouse lady investors, if you want to find me, just go to my website, SpartanInvest.com/investing4women. There's a contact form; you can just drop your name in there. And the free gift that we're giving away is a comprehensive market report on Birmingham because many people just want to know about the market, but they don't know how to find out the details. I get all the information from the Birmingham Business Journal, so it's not Maureen telling you: it's the city telling you about the city itself.

You can find that through our website at spartaninvest.com. Look for me and fill in that contact form.

Moneeka: That's awesome. Thank you for that. Okay, are you ready for our three rapid-fire questions?

Maureen: I am. Go girl.

Moneeka: Let's do it. So Maureen, tell us a super tip on getting started in real estate investing.

Maureen: My super tip is to network. Get off of the couch, disconnect from cable, and get out there and meet people. Go to real estate investment groups, read books, learn, learn, learn. Never stop learning.

Moneeka: Awesome. And then what's a strategy on being successful in real estate investing?

Maureen: Masterminds. It doesn't have to be the paid ones. There are non-paid Masterminds out there. You can start your own Mastermind and invite those beautiful minds in your community that you know are successful in that space, whether it's commercial or residential. Create a Mastermind, invite them in, invite them to lunch, invite them into your home, pick their brain. So, network, network, network, and mastermind.

Moneeka: I love that. Okay, and then tell us one daily practice that you do, Maureen, that you would say contributes to your personal success.

Maureen: There's two. The two most powerful words in any language are, "I am . . ." What you fill in the blank with after those two words is indicative of how you are going to live your life. So, if you say, "I am not smart enough" or "I am not powerful enough" or "No, I can't do that" or "I cannot afford it," then your words will direct your thinking brain to those outcomes. Your mind is a very obedient student. It follows your instructions. Be sure to nourish it with words that will lead you to the life you want, not the one you don't want.

So next time you hear that old narrative running in the background of "I can't, I am not enough," cancel out those thoughts and try on some new ones like, "I am powerful, I am strong, I am a successful real estate investor." I practice saying, "I am ___," and I fill that blank in with all the words that I want to be. So, I would highly recommend you do the same. Put it in writing, put it everywhere, repeat it out loud, who cares who hears it? Because when you declare it, it happens. When you replace your old narrative with a new one, your mind will begin to play the new narrative with the new words, which will lead you to a new outcome. The best way to change your life is to change the words you use every day. Replace "I can't" with "I can." Replace "I don't know how" with "I can figure it out." Words are powerful and words are free. When you change your words, you will change your life.

And then the second point is there's a great app called Insight Timer, meditation for sleep. They're guided meditations for sleep, for accomplishment, for achievement, for power. You can get 10-15 minute meditations that fill your brain with all those good juicy little bits of how you can be powerful and outstanding and amazing.

Moneeka: Ooh, I love that. Insight Timer, awesome. Well, thank you for those tips and thank you so much for all you've shared on the show.

Maureen: My pleasure.

"As I close out this chapter, my core self is searching for the words I can use to impart a lasting change for you, my knowledge-seeking reader. If you are unhappy with your financial life, then

you need to update your financial language. You need to learn the language of money. By learning the language of money through your financial education, you will, with 100% certainty, change your financial future. Things can change when you do, and true change happens when you change your words. Successful business owners, entrepreneurs, and real estate investors like Warren Buffett, Robert Kiyosaki, and Barbara Corcoran did not build their empires on the words 'I can't.' They built their lives on words like 'I can.' And you can too."

~MAUREEN MCCANN

HOW TO BUY AND SELL REAL ESTATE WITHOUT USING CASH OR CREDIT TO CREATE NOW CASH, CASH FLOW, AND WEALTH
WITH CHRIS PREFONTAINE

Moneeka: Today I am so excited to introduce you to our guest, Chris Prefontaine. Chris is a 2 time bestselling author and real estate investor with over 28 years of experience in the field, including 18 years as a builder, realtor, broker-owner, and an investor and coach since 2000.

Chris has always been an entrepreneur, even when he didn't know it! When he was young, he would pull his wagon up to the street corner and sell junk from his closet, or he would buy gum by the pack and sell them by the slice in middle school.

In 1991, Chris began building homes and built 100 homes before starting his own real estate brokerage. He then became a broker-owner and purchased a Realty Executives franchise. In addition to bringing on new agents, he and his own team were selling 100 homes a year before selling to Coldwell Banker in 2000.

Chris, hello, and welcome to the show!

Chris: Thanks for having me on, Moneeka, I appreciate it.

Moneeka: Tell us, what does it mean to buy and sell a home "on terms"?

Chris: Buying "on terms" means "your terms," meaning custom to the person. We buy on lease purchase or owner financing or subject to existing financing. All three of these typically do not require cash, do not require bank loans, do not require credit or you signing personally, so that is what "on terms" means.

Moneeka: People have used these terms a lot on my podcast; could you define all three for us, please?

Chris: Sure, let me give you some examples.

The first is an example of a lease purchase. You are my seller, Moneeka, and I am going to agree with you to either pay your monthly mortgage or some other amount to you if you don't have an underlying debt, and then I am going to install a rent-to-own tenant-buyer. A lease purchase has the seller on one side and the rent-to-own tenant on the other, and we call it a sandwich lease because we are in the middle.

A lease purchase does what? It takes care of the mortgage payment as well as all maintenance and repairs until such time as you agree to cash that house out in 36 months or 48 months or whatever term is agreed upon.

You want to make sure that your tenant-buyer will cash you out ahead of that time frame. That is a lease purchase. Unlike many investors, we put our buyers through a process so they know they can be mortgage ready and receive a game plan to do so. So many mentors teach that it's OK to stick a buyer in the home and have them not be able to purchase so they can go collect another deposit. That may be legally acceptable but we feel it's morally and ethically no acceptable. We set up our buyers to win.

Moneeka: Okay.

Chris: There are many ways to do "owner financing" as your listeners probably know. We do this only when there is no debt on a property though -that's our preference. We structure it so the seller holds the first mortgage and because the payments are monthly principal only—there is no interest—you get massive principal reduction each and every month. We look at those to go out 48 months or more, before the balloon payment is due. How do we make sure the balloon payment gets paid? We do the same thing as on the lease purchase; we put a tenant-buyer in there that has been pre-screened to cash out ahead of that term.

"Subject to" means that I am buying your home, and as my seller, there is an existing debt in place. There is usually no equity there for the owner and they are typically in a more desperate situation, so they are going to sell you the home but they are going to leave the loan in their name.

And I say "typically more desperate" because when people hear "terms," they immediately think anyone willing to sell on terms is desperate or must have problems. Actually, no; we have many sellers that are debt free and just want all the money for their property or for tax or estate planning reasons. It is not just people that are in dire straits. Having said that, with a "subject to," people are having problems, and they want relief usually. So those are the three explanations about "on terms."

Moneeka: What is the difference between the way that you acquire the loan in the first strategy and the last one, lease option and subject to?

Chris: With a lease option, the loan stays in the owner's name and so does the deed; we are just paying their loan directly. We have 50 or 55% of our deals on lease options right now; we are paying the mortgage company directly, but the deed is in the owner's name. The difference on the "subject to" is that we do a closing with our attorney, we do a settlement statement, and we have the deed. Just the loan stays in the owner's name.

When the deed is in our name, what are the advantages? I don't have a clock ticking for an expiration date, I own the home, I can depreciate it, I can control my insurance, and there are other advantages, not just a check and a spread.

Moneeka: It is really interesting the way you do seller financing. What is the advantage to the seller if they are not making any interest?

Chris: Great question! If they ask me, "What is the interest rate?" I say, "What is more important to you, a little bit of interest in this market or do you want a premium on the home instead?"

For example, there was a nice home in Pennsylvania—a 10-acre estate, gorgeous property—the owner was on the market for around $450,000 but could not get it sold with a realtor. If he had sold with a realtor, he probably would have netted somewhere in the low-$400,000s after paying fees and everything. We told him we would give him $460,000 and we would make monthly principal payments. We bump it up a little bit so the owner feels like they are getting all the money they can and they are not having to claim interest income because it is all going to principal. Depending on who it is and their tax situation, there are some advantages as far as interest income.

Moneeka: So you actually pay them more than they are asking; I love that.

Chris: Sometimes.

Moneeka: It is one of my true beliefs that we want to make everybody happy. There are so many people out there trying to lowball the seller, so it is really nice to meet someone who has a strategy that doesn't lowball the seller in that way.

Chris: We get that all the time, people thinking that we are looking to lowball their house. Nope, we are actually looking to pay market value as long as they can work on terms. As an investor calling around, unlike wholesalers or rehabbers, we have little to no competition in most of the states we operate in.

Moneeka: Nice, I love that. Tell us how a new investor can become a full-time real estate entrepreneur.

Chris: There are a couple of things a new investor needs to do. One is to make sure that they have a mentor who they can relate to—because I am not so naive to think I am the only one or that you are the only one, there are other mentors out there. Find someone who you can relate to, someone who is in the niche that you want, and someone who is actually still doing deals. I know it sounds crazy, but you know there are a lot of people teaching about real estate but not doing deals, or not having done deals in years and years. That's scary because the market changes constantly, and you need to be following someone who knows how to adapt and change with it.

Moneeka: I do see that a lot, also.

Chris: Once you have a mentor, then you need an executable plan. There is a huge gap—and I say this in all my videos—between learning and execution. You need a plan to execute, a predictable plan. Those are the two main things to make that transition. You will also need to figure out your personal overhead and what it will take to make the transition; everybody is a little different there.

Moneeka: I talk to lots of people who want to do this full time, but the mentor they get is someone who is not doing the deals like you say.

The other point is that it is not necessary to go full-time. Going full-time may mean doing real estate part-time and then not having to work full-time at all. It depends on what full-time means to you.

Chris: I couldn't agree more. We are teaching people to create three Paydays on each deal that is worth $75,000 per deal on average (that varies around the Country) . If people do one of those deals every other month, they would set up a nice retirement. You don't need 40 hours to do that, you really don't.

Moneeka: That is right.

Chris: In fact, I tell people if you tell me you have 40 hours, I don't know how to fill it; you don't need that much time.

Moneeka: I tell people the same thing. I don't know what you would do with 40 hours dedicated to real estate investing. Go play!

Next, Chris, what are two strategies that you recommend to new investors to prioritize?

Chris: When you are brand new, frankly, I would not try to create a "subject to" or do "owner financing." Because when we put no money down and we are making principal-only payments, we do typically need to pay the owner's transfer tax costs. You can't expect them to come to the table and sell you their home and you not pay anything towards. That, and most states have transfer taxes. Same goes for subject to deals, you're usually not putting anything down and the seller on the subject to deals are usually financially strapped so you're paying transfer tax and misc closing costs.

I would stick with the lease purchase or an offshoot of lease purchase because there is very little risk to you, if any. The offshoot is to do a lease purchase and once you find your buyer, assign them to your seller. We call that an AO (Assign Out). These are two very simple strategies without getting into risk. If a real estate investor is new, I would start with those two.

Moneeka: I love that you talk about keeping it low risk because that is one of my high priorities: I like to build wealth, but I want to keep myself covered.

Chris: You have to.

Moneeka: I don't like high risk. Speaking of which, let's talk about the 2008 real estate debacle. How did you deal with that, and how can people prepare for the future? Because I know people who feel a lot of fear and 2008 is still very fresh in their minds.

Chris: Well, it is fresh in my mind, like it was yesterday! I want to give a little glimpse, but I won't go into the whole story now—there is a whole chapter in my book, Real Estate on Your Terms because I am pretty candid with what we went through and how people can learn from it. We had 22 or 23 properties, Moneeka, that we had signed personally on—mistake—that were also highly leveraged—mistake. When the market took a nose dive, I had one project that was selling, for example, for $170,000 per unit (it was a 6 unit we converted to condos) but I couldn't sell it for $40,000 or $50,000 within a few months of the crash if my life depended on it.

So, the biggest lesson was exactly what we did to reengineer the business with the family here: we do not sign personally ever, and we do not take out bank loans. All the processes that we do now are because of the 2008 debacle, no doubt. There were huge lessons learned, but I don't regret it because we have a stronger business today. In a market where you are doing owner financing or lease purchase, you are getting principal pay-down every single month, you are not on any loans, and you are not on anything ever. Then you are really hedging yourself and you are protecting yourself. That is as close to recession proof as you could be – the entire TERMS niche is when done properly.

Moneeka: That is an interesting take. You have shared such great valuable information, Chris, thank you.

Chris: Thanks for having me on.

Moneeka: How can my listeners get in touch with you?

Chris: I believe in arming investors with as much information as possible so they can do better in their investing. If you go to our website you will see there are a ton of free resources.

We have a podcast, which you have been on.

Moneeka: Yay!

Chris: We have annual live events, and an online course that will teach you everything you need to get started.

On that page, if you go to the RESOURCES tab, you can get all the resources we give to our coaching clients including where to find money, legal help for entity structuring, lead generation, virtual staffing, and how to get business credit. It's a wealth of information and it's all free.

To get access to all that simply go to **blissfulinvestor.com/Smart.**

Moneeka: Wow! That's a lot of great resources! That is so generous Chris. Thank you for that!

Chris: My pleasure.

Moneeka: Ladies I'd like to add just one more thing. As you know I often take classes from guests that I have on my show. I get so inspired I want to learn more, and I also want to vet them for you ladies. I actually take a lot of courses and most of them I am not able to recommend unfortunately.

Because I love Chris' philosophy, his generosity, and his down-to-earth approach to everything he does, I did take his course. I was gifted the online course (thank you Chris) and was so impressed with it that I actually paid full price for their 3 month training. And all I can say is WOW! I loved the training, the coaching, the community, and how many of us had fabulous success during the coaching period. It was so inspiring to watch his professional, compassionate team take us from knowing nothing to succeeding in getting deals done. I learned so much and would highly recommend working with Chris and his team if you are looking for no or low money down strategies to build your real estate business.

I've personally taken about 5 other courses on this topic, and have reviewed many more. Based on that experience, I can say Chris and his team are the best in the business. So please check them out at **blissfulinvestor.com/Smart.**

Moneeka: Okay, are you ready for our three rapid-fire questions?

Chris: Let's do it.

Moneeka: All right. First, Chris, tell us one super tip on getting started in real estate investing.

Chris: I don't want to sound redundant, but you have got to get a mentor who is actually active and who you can relate to. A lot is going to rely on that relationship.

Moneeka: Nice. Tell us one strategy on being successful in real estate investing.

Chris: Aside from the mentor, I would say it is to have some daily rituals that support what you are trying to accomplish in the business. I mentioned earlier about executing; you have got to have something daily that you are doing that will support the execution of your deals, so you are profitable at some point.

Moneeka: Give me an example.

Chris: A daily ritual would be tied to your daily activities; for example, calling sellers is directly related to how many deals you want to do. I hone this down in my webinar: if you want to do X number of deals, then you need to speak with X number of sellers. To match your goals, you actually need to be getting those numbers out every day; it is not vague or ambiguous. If I want 10 deals, I have got to make X number of calls. Chart the calls every single day and make sure you are hitting that number. It is predictable after that. There is no ambiguity.

Moneeka: Got it. And make it so you don't have to think about it. I know with this, or with anything else, that it might feel hard at first, but then it becomes a habit.

Chris: Yes, for sure, and tackle one new habit at a time and build upon that. Think about just adding one new habit or discipline per month—wow, what a year that will be.

Moneeka: If you put yourself in a situation where you have to think about it every day, you are not going to do it, right?

Chris: Right.

Moneeka: Because then it needs to be a decision every day. But if you have it planned and you have got to do it, then you are not making that decision every day, you just do it. Having it planned makes it a lot easier to take action.

Chris: Absolutely. You have highlighted something really big, Moneeka, and that is to follow the process with blind faith. When you start learning from a mentor, I suggest putting the blinders on and not doubting them or yourself for a full 36 months. When you do that, you'll have an amazing experience.

Moneeka: Thank you for that. Tell us one daily strategy or practice that you do, Chris, that contributes to your personal success.

Chris: This is not anything to do with real estate but I can't start the day without one of three things: a workout—which I did today—yoga, or meditating. I do one of those three, no matter what, or else everything gets off-kilter, in my world anyway.

Moneeka: Nice, I love that. Chris, this has been a great conversation, short and to the point and full of amazing information; thank you so much.

Chris: I had fun and I appreciate being on.

> *"I don't care what industry or profession you are in, if you'd like huge success here's the simple formula: Find someone doing what you want to do, achieving what you want to achieve and connect with them and follow them for 36 months with blinders on - no deviating, not distractions, no shiny object syndrome - 100% coachable for 36 months. You will have an amazing experience."*
> ~CHRIS PREFONTAINE

ON THE SUBJECT OF SUBJECT TO
– THE MOMMY STRATEGY
WITH CRYSTAL MEWHORTER

Moneeka: Today, I am so excited to welcome to the show my friend and coach, Crystal Mewhorter. Crystal is the owner of CGN Homebuyers, a successful real estate investing company with a twist. Crystal and her husband, Dan, like to share their business model created by the needs of their customers.

They teach individuals how to invest their funds safely, securely, and at very high rates of return . . . typically tax-free. They assist people in selling homes that cannot sell traditionally and very often sell to individuals that cannot acquire a traditional mortgage. Then they pay for the new owners' credit repair and coach them through to home ownership.

This business was built by a single mom raising two small children, working exorbitant hours and failing to experience any kind of quality of life. Today, Crystal is retired from her J-O-B, drives her kiddos to school, and has been a room mother for several years (which she has so much fun at). She also loves helping her family and her community. She has earned a PRISM Life Design certification, coaches real estate investing, and truly knows and lives financial freedom.

Crystal, thank you so much for coming on the show! How are you?

Crystal: I'm fantastic. Thank you for having me, Moneeka.

Moneeka: So, I just want to let everybody know, Crystal is one of my coaches. She has created a strategy that I like to call the "mommy strategy" because it's a strategy that really comes from her heart and does good in the world.

She's personally training me how to do this, and I just wanted her to share it with all of you ladies because I think you're going to love it. I know how many of you are moms, really wanting to do the right thing out there for your communities, for the people that you're buying from, and also for your children and your families and yourself, of course.

I'm so impressed with Crystal, her knowledge, her success, her heart, and her willingness to share. She does about 70 of these deals per year. That's a lot. So, Crystal, thank you so much joining us today. Could you tell us a little bit about your story? It's so impressive, and I want everybody to know where you came from.

Crystal: Sure, I'd love to tell my story. I feel like it's important for people to know who I am and my background so that they know, without a doubt, that they can do this, no matter what their current situation.

I actually started investing in 1996, really traditionally. I would buy a house using a bank loan. I would move into the house, rehab it, and then sell it. Typically, I'd hold onto it for a year just so that I would avoid short-term capital gains. Then I'd move on and do that with the next property.

At the exact same time, I was an occupational therapist in a leadership role. So, I was working a more-than-full-time job while I was doing my real estate investing. That's why it made sense to do my investing that way. Somewhat late in life, I decided to finally get married and have children.

Right around 2007, just before the market started to make its big shift, I sold my last house in a bidding war with the idea in mind that I would focus on my career. I thought that's where my time and energy should be spent. I didn't need to be having all these extra things going on, moving from house to house, especially with a husband and planning to have children.

So, I stepped away, and I really focused my energy on my career. I was blessed to have two beautiful children. My son Gavin, who is the oldest, and my daughter Nevaeh. As we all know . . . the best laid plans don't always go as planned! When Nevaeh was a baby, I became a single mom. Obviously, that was not part of my plan, and at that point, I needed to make some very serious decisions.

I was having someone drop them off at my office every day at the end of the day, and many nights we'd be there until about nine o'clock at night, and I would be trying to get everything together. I'd have this toddler and this infant and we were just trying to get home.

There was a night that was really a turning point for me. I was driving home late and I drove my little boy through a drive-through to get him something to eat, which I said I'd never ever do. That was just off the table, not an option for me. However, here I was feeding my toddler fast food and at a ridiculous hour when he should be home and in bed fast asleep. I knew so deep within me that something needed to change. My life just didn't make sense. I wasn't spending time with my kids, they were being raised by daycare (a great program, albeit), but I didn't have them with me. Not only did we not have any quality of life as our new small family unit, but I had no quality of life at all.

I took some time to reflect, looking at my resources, what had served me in the past, and decided that real estate investing had been really good to me. I felt that if I could do something with that, maybe I could change this situation and finally get away from the space where I couldn't spend time with my little ones. At the time, I wasn't able to get involved in any school activities, even the little things they were already doing and participating in. I knew as it progressed, it was going to be a difficult situation. Being completely transparent, financially, I was raising them on only my income. My dream had been to send them to private school. Obviously, with only one income, no matter how good, that was not looking very promising, either.

At that point, I started to look into getting some education, knowing that the real estate market had shifted and I was going to have to look at some different strategies. It was clear to me that I couldn't move my kids into a new house every year; that simply would not make sense. From this simple moment of awareness, and a couple of small key steps, I started to develop a business. I hired a coach and mentor and then was able to actually retire full-time from my career. It didn't happen immediately, but after working both careers for a while, I went from my full-time career to full-time in real estate investing because the business had become so successful.

At the end of all this, I actually did meet a lovely man and we were married just a couple of years ago. The amazing part was that I was able to create this whole business, and now he actually works full-time for our business as well. I have all the freedom that I want as far as what I want to do with my time. I spend a lot of that with my children and my husband. We travel all the time because we can work from anywhere. We get to make decisions in our life that are based on what we'd really like to do and not what we absolutely have to do, and not what somebody is telling me I have to do.

It's just been the most amazing ride. That's why I love coaching, because I get to give back and share with people that if someone like myself can do this, so can they! And there was nothing that I had that made me special. I'm just like anybody else. I was out there, a struggling single mom and now here I am.

Moneeka: I love how you talk about how you went full-time, because I know you don't actually work full-time.

Crystal: Okay, well, that's relative.

Moneeka: It's part-time/full-time.

Crystal: Yeah, it is.

Moneeka: What I really love is that you feel like you've been able to truly design your life. These are words that especially millennials use all the time. "Design your life, design your life, design your life." But it's according to whatever somebody else thinks designing your life looks like. And what I really love is how you support people to design what they truly believe is what their life should look like, according to their own feelings.

I know several times I've called Crystal when we had a coaching call, and I'd say, "Hey, I'm in New Orleans next week, I don't think I can talk on Tuesday" because I want to spend time with my husband. After all, that's why I'm on vacation. And there's never a reprimand or any judgment around that. Crystal really understands that designing life is about creating the life that's blissful for me. Not what someone else says I should be designing. Right?

Crystal: Absolutely. And I think that's where a lot of people get caught up. We're so used to the mentality of, "I am what I do in my work space, and that generally means working for someone else . . . what I do is who I am." And we let that define us, and then someone else is telling us who we are each step of the way. So, while we think we're managing our own lives, very minimally are we doing that. Certainly, with most positions, you couldn't decide that tomorrow you're going to take a vacation or completely change direction with your position, your role in the company, or take a different path. Working for someone else generally means that you are helping to move them toward achievement of their "Why" and their larger vision. That's the beauty of having your own business, being an entrepreneur and truly designing your life. Your "Why" is what's important, fuels your vision, and ultimately leads you to living out your TRUE purpose.

The focus of my coaching certification is: how do you design your life? How do we create that vision, that future? You need to be able to see your future as you want it to be and tailor it to you.

Moneeka: Because most entrepreneurs design a business that eventually owns them. And I think you're a perfect example of designing a life where you own the business and the business takes care of you. It certainly doesn't run your life, which is really amazing.

So, the strategy that you and I have been talking so much about and I'm so excited to share with my audience, is this strategy called Subject-To. This is what I call the "mommy strategy." Could you tell us what Subject-To is?

Crystal: Subject-To simply means that you are purchasing a property, "subject to" the existing mortgage. The investor takes title to the property, while the existing note stays in the seller's name. Therefore, it is not an assumption. You're taking over the payments for the existing note, but you are not personally guaranteeing the debt.

Moneeka: Talk a little bit about the difference between assuming the mortgage and taking over it. Because I know that the banks have a clause that the loan cannot be assumed. So, talk to us a little bit about the difference.

Crystal: Just for clarification, assumption and having loans that you could assume was actually commonplace-"ish" for a while, especially on some of the VA loans. Now, you see it very, very rarely. For the most part, you can't assume loans anymore.

The difference is that in Subject-To, you are creating a contract where you're taking responsibility for making those payments, but the mortgage still remains in the seller's name. When you do an assumption, you're actually assuming the debt. You're personally guaranteeing the debt.

Moneeka: The very first time I heard about this, I thought, "Why would anybody sell you their house and keep the loan?" Could you just address that really quickly? Because I know that's what's going through people's minds.

Crystal: That's what goes through everybody's mind. Mine as well, initially. The first time I had ever heard about it, I thought that just seems absolutely ridiculous. However, after several years working with individuals, it is perfectly clear to me why people would do this. People that are willing to sell a property and keep the loan in their name have a significant need. Generally, these individuals want debt relief and stress relief. Something is happening in their life that they aren't in a position to make an alternate decision. They have to do something, and this is a way for them to move on. Those reasons can be various. You've heard investors mention the term "motivated" all the time. What they mean by "motivated" is somebody that has something that's happening in their life that's causing them to need some help.

Moneeka: Got it. So where do you find these people that might consider a Subject-To?

Crystal: There's a lot of ways to find people that are motivated to sell in this fashion. One of my favorite strategies is FSBO (For Sale by Owners), where you are working directly with the seller(s). I actually have a team that works on contacting people that are trying to sell their home themselves.

Additionally, I work with about 10 different strategies, but we don't need to talk about them all here. So, FSBOs are a great place to start.

Moneeka: Okay, great. And like you said, there are 10 different strategies that we can use for that. FSBOs are probably the lowest hanging fruit, right?

Crystal: That's true, and the "resource" is free. I think that's really important to remember, because when I started, the last thing that I had was a ton of extra cash to go looking for alternate ways to advertise and to connect with sellers. So, I didn't have a lot of ways to reach out. This was a great strategy for me, and this was how I bought the initial part of my portfolio—all straight FSBO.

Moneeka: It's so interesting, Crystal, because there are so many strategies that say, "Go talk to the FSBOs." I remember when I actually did a "for sale by owner," I got bombarded by all these people. And I thought, "What in the world, what is going on?" And now of course, I'm in this industry, so I know what the heck is going on. But what's interesting to me is that it worked for you.

There are a lot of different people coming at these FSBOs, but it's really about how you do that approach. And this is another thing that I think a woman brings to the table, this heart-centered approach of, "I'm here to help you and solve a problem for you." And so yeah, it's free, and the reason it works is because of what you as a woman can bring to the table. It's a "Let's work this out" strategy, right?

Crystal: Absolutely. It's all about the conversation and connection.

Moneeka: Which leads us to the next point. So, talk about that initial first conversation.

Crystal: During the initial conversation, I am reaching out to a "for sale by owner" client, and of course, like you said, they've heard from a dozen investors and they're over it. Ultimately, the first thing that I want to do, is reach out and just talk to them and truly let them see that I'm simply a person, just like them. I feel it's important to actually have a conversation and get to know each other a little bit.

I genuinely think that that's the part where most people fall apart, if you will. They're too interested in trying to make a deal. You're not going to make a deal in the first two and a half seconds, so you need to just drop that. Have a conversation with these people, get to know them, let them get to know a little bit about you. Then I'm going to ask them questions about their house.

I want to know what it is that they're trying to accomplish. They're trying to sell this house, but in what time period and what is it that they really need? Some people absolutely have to cash out because they have to get another mortgage and they have to move on. Other people already have another house, they're just over this, they've been a landlord, or they're in a hurry. A lot of people simply need to move on, and they don't have time to get it sold. Many other individuals are "upside down" on their mortgage, so that's why they're selling for sale by owner.

The first conversation is really, let's get to know each other. Let's find out what it is that they're trying to accomplish.

Moneeka: Perfect. And then what are some of the objections that you come up against? Give me like your top one or two.

Crystal: One of the first objections, of course, is really they don't want to deal with an investor. So, people have a really bad sense of what that even means. So, when they first find out, they'll often say things like, "Wait a minute, are you an investor?"

"Yeah, absolutely, I'm an investor."

Then you have to work through that piece. How am I going to help that person to understand who it is that they're dealing with and that I'm not like other investors that they may have had to deal with that left a bad taste in their mouth?

I'm Crystal, who cares what's going on, who has a whole family to support with this. So needless to say, I want to make sure that I can convey that I do what I say I'm going to do and they're in the right hands.

The second objection is, "Wait a minute, wait a minute, you're going to leave this in my name. How do I know you're going to pay, and what happens if you don't?" This one is a biggie. Whenever I'm training someone on how to do this, I'm always trying to explain to them, "The sellers need to know that they can trust you and that you're establishing a relationship with one another. They need to know who you are. It's really important to show them who you are."

One easy way to share your credibility is by leveraging social media. Social media is a huge component of today's society. So, I'm going to send them right out there to take a look at our company. "Look me up, here's our websites, Facebook page, Pinterest, Twitter, Google us, etc. This is my information. If I'm not doing what I'm supposed to be doing, you're going to see it." Along this same vein, I make it clear that if I am not supporting my obligations, then I wouldn't have a business, and that's how I keep a roof over my family's head.

Secondly, it's important that they understand that everything is done at our attorney's office. Finally, I make them aware of the "worst case scenario." If I don't pay, they get the house back, in better condition than when they started, since I complete any repairs and upgrades when I take possession.

Moneeka: You actually had a really good one-liner that you told me one time when you were coaching me, about when they say, "How do I know you're going to pay?" Do you remember what that was?

Crystal: "We're a family-owned company. The name of the company is C for Crystal, G for my son Gavin, and N for my daughter Neveah, homebuyers. In order to keep a roof over my family's head, I need to make sure that I stand by my obligations. And if I don't do that, then we don't have a roof over our heads. I can't take care of my children."

Moneeka: That's so powerful. That's the one that I was looking for. And it's just allowing people to see your own pain point. Because you're basically saying, "You know what, this is my livelihood, and without this, I can't support my children." That's your pain point. And if you allow them to see your pain point, that you're real, that you're human, that really, really helps to build trust, I think.

Yeah, and it was really fun at one point, Crystal let me sit down with her while she was making phone calls to prospects. And it was really interesting to hear the really angry, "Are you an investor? Wait a minute, I don't want to talk to investors." And how she so just gently and beautifully turned that around until they were laughing on the other line. I thought, "OMG, that's like magic. She's amazing, really."

This is another thing that I really want to say, Crystal is this really beautiful, soft person. She's very feminine in her business. And I think that a lot of people, when you're watching someone like me or like Crystal, you might say, "Oh well, they're not go-getters. They're not hustlers. They're not going to get the best deal."

There are all these impressions about a feminine leader in this business. The truth is, it's because we show up this way, in such a different way, that we stand out and why people want to do business with us. So, this is another example, ladies, of what's possible when you really step into your feminine in this business and really tune into those resources of who you are as a woman and what you bring to the table.

I think Crystal is a beautiful example of that. I've really appreciated her coaching because of that, because she speaks the kind of language that I want to speak when I'm talking to people.

Crystal: I think it's important to recognize that when you bring your genuine self (and we all know this intuitively, we just do), it shows through. I can tell you more than just a handful of times, I have gotten the deal where there's a bunch of other investors involved because people make the comment, "Oh, well I just really like you. I'd really like to work with you," and I might not have even come up with the best offer. I truly believe it's because I've taken the time to show them who I am and to get to know who they are. I am coming from a space of clearly and completely understanding them. And I'm speaking to that. I'm sharing that with them. "Okay, great. I really look forward to doing this so that we can help you do **X**." I'm not like, "Okay, great, let's get this done." Which is what most people do. They're just in such a hurry and they're just thinking about the numbers and the next step. Do I think about numbers? Of course I do. That's my responsibility. However, first and foremost, I'm thinking about what this is going to do for this person and then, subsequently, what does it do for me and my family? How does that all work together so there's a complete win-win?

Moneeka: Again, it's not giving the win-win lip service. It really is win-win. If it's not a win for them, you won't do the deal. If it's not a win for you, you won't do the deal. You're not giving this lip service. It's not pretty languaging. It's actually happening.

Crystal: I have turned away more than a few people because of that. For instance, just looking at the information, if I notice they have considerable equity, and then they tell me they want to be able to purchase another home in the next 6 months, then I've told them straight out, "Oh no, you have a good amount of equity and want the ability to purchase in the near future, this wouldn't be the right thing for you. This just wouldn't make good sense. You need to do **X**." Understanding that how I purchase and their objectives need to match. What I do is going to affect their plans.

So, I just want to make sure that everything looks good for everybody involved. I don't ever want anyone to think, "Oh my goodness, I wish I'd never done this."

Moneeka: That's how I feel about it, too. I don't want people to think, "Oh, I just got taken advantage of, but I was in such a tight situation." I just don't ever want anybody to say that about me, either.

Tell us a little bit about how you can help them. I know that you've got a little bit of a process around this.

Crystal: I sure do. Let's say that the individual that we're talking about is in a possible pre-foreclosure situation or maybe in foreclosure. And so that's why they're selling it for sale by owner. They're in a big hurry, obviously. These are individuals that I often encounter. Once I discover they are behind on payments and either in foreclosure or facing the possibility, the first question I ask them is, "Do you want to keep your house?" So, my first question isn't, "Ok great, I want to buy it, let's move on." My first question is, "Do you want to keep your house?" if I am aware that there's a problem.

At the first instance that I'm made aware that they're behind on their payments or that they're going down that road, I'm going to start walking them through that process. "Okay, these are the things that you need to be aware of. These are the things that you need to look into. These are the things you need to avoid," so that I can protect them as best as possible. Because, unfortunately, there are not a lot of people out there that are willing to do that.

If at that point, they still need to sell, then perfect. I definitely want to help them and I'll get that completed for them. We'll get the house sold, we'll do the purchase. However, if I can help them in any way. I'll even look into what their resources might be, so that they can keep their home— then I want to help them to keep their home. I provide an entire list of those resources, go over it with them, and I actually send it to them. It's not just, "Hey, quick, can you write down this website? Here, you might want to write that." I send it to them. I just say, "Hey, great. Do you have an email that I can send this to?" And I've actually even gone as far as to drop it off at their home so that they have the paper and can look at it if they don't have an email or access to email.

Moneeka: Well, and they're probably getting a lot of ugly emails. In the old days, we used to get a lot of ugly mail. Now we get ugly mail and ugly telephone calls. So, they're probably staying out of communication a little bit, too. And their mind is kind of all over the place and they're frustrated and scared, possibly, and stressed out. So, to have somebody actually pay attention to trying to actually help in a way that's just being of service is really going to make a big impact, I think.

Crystal: Absolutely. We know that fear has many manifestations. Sadly, one of the most common, especially in a position like that, is that they're paralyzed. So they're not doing anything and they're not looking at anything and they're not talking to anybody. If you can give them some avenues to start to get a little information and a spark of hope as to what might be available to them, then obviously, that makes a tremendous difference in this process.

Moneeka: Perfect. Tell us a little bit about what the Subject-To process looks like.

Crystal: It's probably one of the most simplistic processes, if you will, in regard to real estate transactions. It's really pretty straightforward. Through communication with the seller, you need to come to an agreement that they are willing to do subject-to and on the price. It's necessary that you get information regarding the mortgage balance, lender, and payments. Your attorney draws up the contracts for you to purchase the house. The process is that I need to have obviously the mortgage information. A title search must be complete to assure that you have clear title. Once all of the due diligence is complete, you take title and the mortgage remains in the seller's name. At this time, you control the property and will start making payments.

Moneeka: Perfect. Crystal, can you tell people how they can get in touch with you?

Crystal: You can reach me at my personal email, ursuccesscoachcrystal@gmail.com, and you can use the link blissfulmommystrategy.com to get in touch with me there as well.

Moneeka: Great. So, at blissfulinvestor.com/crystal, I know that Crystal has a free gift that she's giving. Could you tell us about that?

Crystal: I am giving away a free PDF of the list of resources that I actually share with my own potential sellers. You can take this, use it, share it with them, and offer that level of assistance to your clients, all the while building relationship and rapport.

Moneeka: Talk about taking your business to the next level, that's amazing. Thank you so much. That's awesome.

Crystal: It's my pleasure.

Moneeka: Are you ready for our three rapid-fire questions?

Crystal: I'm ready.

Moneeka: Okay, Crystal, tell us one super tip on getting started in real estate investing.

Crystal: So my super tip would be you have to hire somebody that you trust to help you learn this process, to learn to be an investor. Absolutely, you need a coach and mentor. Make sure that it's somebody that you can trust in and believe in.

Moneeka: Thank you for that. And what's one strategy on being successful in real estate investing?

Crystal: Real estate investing is about relationships. To me, to really become a successful real estate investor, you need to know and own that piece. You need to understand that this is a relationship. That there's nothing one-sided about any of this, and that when you're looking at each and every situation, there's more than yourself involved. You're interacting with a person, and the quicker you can learn that in this business, the faster and far more successful you'll be.

Moneeka: Thank you. And that's what I always say, too, is so many people think it's a numbers business. And like you say, we do need to know the numbers, but it really is a people business. It really is about the relationships.

Crystal: It is, unquestionably.

Moneeka: And tell us one daily practice that you would say contributes to your personal success.

Crystal: My personal success, I feel, hinges 100% on my morning routine. I arise early. I'm usually up by 4:30. I meditate, I read for 30 minutes, I have a gratitude practice, and I do yoga all before I wake everybody else up and get the day started. Without that, I don't think that my mind would be right, and I wouldn't be in the right personal space to be able to serve all the clients and deal with the things that I need to in the way that I should. I really do believe that that is the basis for my success.

Moneeka: Thank you for those. That's amazing. Crystal, thank you so much for joining us and for all that you've shared. I've super appreciated it.

Crystal: It's my pleasure, and I thank you for having me on.

"You don't have to be extraordinary to begin, but you do have to begin, or you'll always be ordinary."
~CRYSTAL MEWHORTER

CREATE PASSIVE INCOME IN REAL ESTATE WITHOUT RENTERS, REHABS, RENOVATIONS, OR RODENTS
WITH MARK PODOLSKY

Moneeka: Armed with only $3,000, gut-wrenching fear, and absolutely no real estate experience, Mark bought his first few parcels of raw land in 2001.

Today, Mark is the owner of Frontier Properties, a very reputable and successful land investing company, and has been buying and selling land full time since 2001. By focusing on working smart, not hard, he has completed over 5,000 land deals with an average ROI of over 300% on cash flips, and over 1,000% on the deals he sells with financing terms.

Prior to his land investing success, Mark had a high-stress, soulless corporate job and felt trapped in a state of solo-economic dependency (i.e., his income stopped as soon as he stopped working).

Escaping solo-economic dependency changed Mark's life in so many positive ways that he decided to teach, coach, and mentor others to help them achieve their financial goals.

Even though Mark invests a lot of his time helping others, he stays actively involved in running his land investing business and is dedicated to teaching the most current and relevant "real world" land investing methods to his students.

Moneeka: So Mark, thank you for coming and joining us on the show. I'm so excited to talk to you today. How are you doing?

Mark: Moneeka, thank you so much. Everything's great. Thank you. Thanks for having me.

Moneeka: My pleasure. I just I had so much fun chatting with you on your show about blissful real estate investing, and I am so excited today to find out more about what you do. So let's just jump right in.

You sent me some talking points like automation systems, delegation, so let's—

Mark: I know. It's so geeky, I'm so geeky, Moneeka.

Moneeka: You are such a geek, and this geek with this amazing voice. That's not normal, but we really appreciate it.

So tell us about what you do and how it works for you, and tell us about your systems and automation and delegation and all that cool stuff.

Mark: Sure. It might be easier if I just walk you through the model.

Moneeka: I'd love that.

Mark: So Moneeka, you're in Silicon Valley, right?

Moneeka: Correct.

Mark: Okay, so let's say I'm going to get the delinquent tax list from Moneeka. And obviously, oh my gosh, Moneeka Sawyer owes $200 in back taxes on this 10-acre parcel in a county in Texas. And so, Moneeka, you're advertising two things to me. Number one, you have no emotional attachment to that raw land. You live in Silicon Valley, the property is in Texas. Two, you're advertising to me that you are distressed in some way. When we don't pay our taxes, pay towards something, we don't value it anymore.

So, either you don't value the property anymore, maybe you've lost your job, maybe there's something going on in your life, who knows? But you haven't paid your taxes, so that means something's going on.

So what I'll do is I'll look at the list for the last 12 to 18 months on those 10-acre parcels in Texas. And all I'm going to do then is take the lowest comparable and divide by four, and that's going to get me what Warren Buffet would call a 300% margin of safety. So I'm going to actually send you an offer on that 10-acre parcel.

So for our purposes, let's say the lowest comp is $10,000, the most I'm going to pay for your 10-acre parcel is $2,500. Now in reality, 3 to 5% of people will accept this "top dollar" offer. And you, who has $200 in back taxes, you know that eventually you're just going to lose this property. You have no emotional attachment to the property, so you accept the offer.

After you accept it, then I go through due diligence. Number one, I have to make sure you actually own the property. Number two, I have to make sure that you only owe $200 in back taxes, not $2,000, killing my margin. Number three, I have to make sure that there's ingress and egress, or legal access. I have a whole checklist. I want to make sure there's no breaks in the chain of title. I want to make sure that there's no liens or encumbrances. All these wonderful things just to make sure everything is kosher.

And then what we'll do is we'll buy that property from you for $2,500. And now, I have at least one built-in buyer to immediately buy that property from me for over $10,000. Do you know who that is?

Moneeka: Who?

Mark: The neighbors. I send out neighbor letters saying, "Hey, before I go to the open market, here's your opportunity. Protect your privacy, protect your views, expand your holdings and acquire this parcel."

Oftentimes the neighbors will buy it. And the way that I'll sell it (and this is where the magic comes in), is I'm going to sell it on owner financing. So I'm going to get a $2,500 down payment. So I'm going to get my money out on the down payment, depending on the parcel. And then I'm just going to get a car payment, let's say $449 a month at 9% interest over the next eight years.

So essentially, it's a one-time sale. I get this passive income every single month of $449 a month at 9% interest. But Moneeka, I've got no renters, no rehabs, no renovations, no rodents. And by not dealing with a tenant, I am exempt from owners' real estate legislation like Dodd-Frank—RESPA with the SAFE Act. And so the game that we play is create enough of this passive income where it exceeds my fixed expenses and then I'm working because I want do, not because I have to. That's what I do.

Moneeka: Wow! Oh, my God. That's amazing, Mark. And the way that you just put that in one little capsule for us—that was amazing.

Mark: Thank you. And then the geeky part of it is that I can do this from anywhere in the world. All I need is an inexpensive computer and an internet connection. By using software today, 90% of my business is done online. It's absolutely incredible. It's the best time ever to be in business.

Moneeka: Wow, so you don't visit the properties or meet the neighbors or meet the seller or any of those things?

Mark: I can't tell you the last time I physically went out to go look at a piece of property. What we'll do is we'll hire somebody. Let's say it's an area that I'm unfamiliar with. We'll hire somebody on Craigslist and do a local Craigslist gig: we'll give them our property report, and we'll send them out there. We'll have them take pictures, shoot video, and report back to us. Are the neighbors dumping? What's the road like? Is it rock? Is it gravel? Is a dirt? Is it paved? What's compelling about the property? Here are the GPS coordinates. How long did it take for you to find the property?

And so, we really get a good sense of what it's going to be like for that buyer when they go out to actually physically inspect the property. So we outsource that, and that's typically about 50 bucks.

Moneeka: Wow! And do you do specific places? How do you pick the areas that you look for?

Mark: Moneeka, nobody wakes up and thinks to themselves, "Boy, I'd really like to own some raw land today in Minnesota"—unless you've been in Minnesota. The states I focus on are going to be California, Nevada, Arizona, New Mexico, Colorado, Texas, Oregon, Washington, Florida. These are fast-growing states. These are states that have inexpensive raw land. And so I want the biggest buyer pool possible, and I also want the biggest pool of potential deals possible. And within those states, I mean, there's billions of acres of raw land available.

Moneeka: I have to confess, I'm kind of speechless. This has never happened on my podcast. Like I don't know what to say. Just WOW!

Mark: Yeah, I mean, the thing is that it's the most unsexy real estate niche there is, because you're not going to go on HGTV or the DIY Network and see Flip This Land. It's Mark in front of his computer. Like it's the most boring thing ever. Like, "Oh, there's a piece of raw land."

If I go to a party, Moneeka, and tell people what I do, they're like, "Oh." There's no other question after I tell them, "I invest in raw land." I just get blurry stares. So it's a really unsexy niche. There's almost no one doing it in a massive market.

Moneeka: This is so interesting to me! So first of all, it's really funny that you say that it's an unsexy niche. That's something that I say all the time. You know what I do, this buy-and-hold thing, is so not sexy. It's not the fix-and-flip. It's not the wholesaling. It's not cool and exciting. But I will say this, Mark, what you and I make is pretty sexy, so whatever.

Mark: Moneeka, you're building your wealth slowly.

Moneeka: Every moment counts.

Mark: But in our culture today, we all want it right now. And unfortunately, that's just not the way it works. Like I love that we're playing this sort of boring long game and building our net worth daily.

Moneeka: Yeah, that's right. Because making it work is better than being exciting, at least in business. We can do whatever we want in our normal lives. But in business, it's all about making it work in a way that really supports your life.

May I ask, if the neighbors don't want to buy the properties, what do you do?

Mark: I'm going to sell this property in 30 days or less. So the way that I'm going to do it is I'm going to make it irresistible. If the neighbors pass, then I'll go to my buyers list. We've got a really big buyers list. But if you're a newbie and you need a buyers list, then you're going to go to a little website that' Moneeka, you've probably never heard of called Craigslist. It's the 10th most trafficked website in the United States.

Moneeka: Oh, my gosh, I've never heard of that one!

Mark: And using software and automation, I can post about 120 ads by pressing a button. Then also, we use the same thing with Facebook buy/sell groups. So we'll go to these niche buy/sell groups, and we're going to sell that way. Now, there's also landmodo.com, landsofamerica.com, landflip.com, landhub.com. Let's just call them the "lands." So these are websites devoted to selling raw land.

Moneeka: Okay, very cool. You sent me something about geekpay. Tell me a little bit about that.

Mark: Okay, so now what happens is, let's say that you've got a hundred borrowers making payments of let's say $449 a month. So Moneeka, that's a really difficult thing to manage. And what **geekpay** does, it automates that process. So essentially, we're going to get our down payment and then we have a promissory note. Then, we're going to have the software do the amortization table, do the calculations of interest and principal. And it's also going to automate the notifications to the borrower. "We received your payment" or "Oh no, your payment was late" or "Oh, no, your payment bounced this month."

And what's nice about geekpay, and what's really lowered my default rate in half, is that if the ACH fails or the checking account on file fails, we can have multiple accounts as backups. So we can use a credit card on file as backup. And so **GeekPay** then will hit their credit card, and if their ACH and their credit card both fail, I know I've got a really weak buyer. And most likely, I'm going to have to resell that property.

But because we use land contracts, there's no cost to foreclose. I keep the down payment. I keep the monthly payments. If they don't cure their default within 30 days, I keep all the payments and I just resell the property to someone else. I get a new down payment, and I extend out my note, increasing my ROI even more.

But the beautiful thing about **geekpay** is it eliminated two really big headaches for me. The first phone call was, "Hey, Mark, what's my current balance?" Well, now the borrower can go in and see their current balance without having to call me. The second annoying call was, "Hey, Mark, how do I make a prepayment this month?" And they can go in now and make a prepayment at any time as well. Because my philosophy is: I can always make more money, but I can't get more time. So anything that'll save me time, I want to invest in.

Moneeka: I love how **GeekPay** helps you to automate everything. Automation is a critical key to bliss because it gives you time freedom, just like you said. How can my ladies find out more about GeekPay?

Mark: I created a couple of links especially for your group Moneeka. To get more information about GeekPay just go to **https://blissfulinvestor. com/geekpayinfo**. If anyone wants to look at what the options, features, and benefits of **GeekPay** are, just go to **https://blissfulinvestor.com/geek-payoptions**.

Moneeka: Thank you for that Mark! So, tell me what are the terms usually of your notes?

Mark: It just depends on the property. So typically, it's going to go anywhere from 3 years to 30, depending on how expensive that property is. So I would say the average note is probably about 8 to 10 years.

Moneeka: And that's mostly focused on making the payment really achievable and an instant yes for people. So you structure the time frame to make it easy?

Mark: Exactly. So for every thousand dollars I invest in a piece of raw land, I'm going to make that note at least $100 per month. So just for easy math, if I invested $3,000, the minimum I would take as a monthly payment is $300 a month. These aren't big Moneeka Sawyer deals; I mean, these are small deals. So, I don't have to go out and get private money or outside investors or anything like that. It's very easy to start with very little capital.

Moneeka: Nice. Okay, very cool. Wow! Tell me about the Dirt Rich book.

Mark: Dirt Rich is the first book I've ever written. And I thought, well, I've got podcasts and I've got all these things, like why not write a book? I was tired of having people on my podcast constantly saying, "I wrote a book." And I kept thinking, "Oh, okay."

So it was kind of an ego-driven thing, but as I got to writing it, I really enjoyed the process of it. Dirt Rich really breaks down my story. It also discusses my crash in 2010 and this epiphany I had about what's really important to me in life. And then it's also a "how to" book.

So it's called Dirt Rich: How One Ambitiously Lazy Geek Created Passive Income in Real Estate Without Renters, Renovations, and Rehabs.

Moneeka: Or rodents.

Mark: Or rodents. Yeah, so it really tells my story in embarrassing detail as well as talking a lot about the details of what we just discussed in the model.

Moneeka: Could you talk about the book that you're writing now?

Mark: Let's say, for example, that you've got all this passive income, you're a one-percenter and yet happiness eludes you. Because I had all those things, but I was so unhappy. My relationships were frayed. Things were not going well. And so this new book is more about the principles that one needs to cultivate happiness so it doesn't elude them. The real meaning of purpose and success.

Right now, the title is Coax the Cat, with the metaphor being that if you want to get a cat to sit on your lap, it's not going to happen if you chase after the cat. You have to create the right environment. Using the metaphor that if you want success in life, you have to create the right environment and have the right principles.

These principles are gratitude, humility, authenticity, continual improvement, embracing the suck, being comfortable not being comfortable, going outside of your comfort zone, looking for growth. Have this internal metric of success. Then, no matter what happens, when you have this environment, the cat just wants to come up and sit on your lap. You'll find that success just flows way, way easier and things become more joyful. It's still effortful, but it feels more effortless.

Moneeka: So for my audience, you can see now why I really wanted Mark on this show. Because I wrote the book Choose Bliss for exactly the same reasons. I was an executive coach for people that had millions of dollars and the nice house and the great wife or husband and the two kids and the white picket fence and the adorable dog and the nice cars, and they had everything—and they were unhappy and miserable.

As a coach, this became my specialty. People really want to be happy in life more than anything else, and when that's eluding you, you need to find what you called it—a sort of inner compass of true happiness. When I wrote Choose Bliss, I wanted to share strategies for finding that, finding your direction to true joy. Because that's really what we're after. We want to be happy.

And people call it all sorts of different things. They call it rich. They call it having the perfect relationship. They call it being able to shop for whatever they want. But in the end, in the very end, it's really about, "Am I happy? Do I matter? Do I matter to me?"

Mark: Absolutely. I would have been your client, for sure.

Moneeka: Yeah. So that's why I feel like we're such a great connect, and I'm so excited for your book to come out! So great. You also just had a workshop, which is all about the land purchase stuff?

Mark: Yeah, we had a two and a half day intensive . . . it's so cool because everything is so virtual now. My whole team's virtual; I work out of my separate air-conditioned garage. And so to get together every quarter with our community and talk about these deals and see people closing deals in real time. Telling stories about how I've done deals and things have changed through the years because I've been doing this now full time since 2001. I've seen so many different scenarios, and it's great for people to have the opportunity to network and ask questions.

I tell them that when they come to boot camp, all the land investing clouds in their heads are going to dissipate. Things will get very clear. And by Sunday, it happens. And it's amazing to see how the room starts off as strangers and they leave as friends by Sunday. And I say it every boot camp: there isn't a person in that room I personally wouldn't have a drink with just on my own. Like just really good, solid people, Moneeka. I'm sure you attract the same type of people.

Moneeka: I do. I'm really, really lucky. I absolutely love my clients. If I could go on vacation with them to Hawaii, I would. I love them. And you've made a really, really good point. I've started to implement two-day live virtual workshops and Masterminds. I've also implemented a shopping day, which is so great for the blissful real estate investors. Because, for mostly women, we like to go shopping, and we like to go shopping for houses. We're not talking shoes and purses, we're talking houses.

So it's really, really fun. And you're right, it's awesome to build a community on the phone. Everybody has really come together to support each other. It's been amazing, and I love them all. And it 10x-ed that community and the relationships as soon as we all got to meet and hang out. So it's such a great way to learn. It's also a great way to build community.

Mark: Oh, yeah. There's nothing like being together like that. I do Zoom Mastermind calls, and there's nothing like being in the same room—the energy is phenomenal. I wish I could do them more, but of course, I've got three kids. My daughter always cries, "Daddy, you're leaving for boot camp again? You're always traveling." I've got friends who are on the road four days a week. I'm around like every day. I take her to school every day.

Moneeka: Yeah, it's all perspective. Even in real estate, it's all perspective. Awesome! Mark, tell us how people can get in touch with you.

Mark: I think the best way is to go to **blissfullandgeek.com**, and they can download for free our passive income blueprint. They can also get The Art of Passive Income podcast each week to their email inbox. There they can hear the amazing interview with Moneeka Sawyer.

If they are loving what we are talking about and eager to take action, they can get more information about our Foundational Training at **https:// blissfulinvestor.com/landgeekladies**.

Moneeka: You rock! That's great. Yes, everybody should download that free gift. I am definitely going to go take a look. I've just been so impressed with how simple you've made this system. It's really awesome. I'm a total systems person because as far as I'm concerned, if you can plug yourself into a system that's aligned with who you are, what your goals are, what your resources are, and it works consistently, then you've definitely got a recipe for success.

Mark: Right, would you call it blissful?

Moneeka: Oh, my gosh, systems are what make everything so much more blissful. I just have to say that that's true!
Alrighty. Are you ready for our three rapid-fire questions?

Mark: Whoa! All right, Moneeka, I'm ready. Should I sit or stand?

Moneeka: Totally as you wish. Here we go. Okay, so Mark, tell us one super tip on getting started in investing in real estate.

Mark: A super tip to getting started in real estate is getting educated first. So I suggest in anything like starting a new endeavor, whether it's a new business or real estate investing, find your Sherpa. Find somebody who's already done what you want to do and have them help you climb that mountain. You'll get there more quickly, more safely, more efficiently. That's where I would first start.
That doesn't mean don't take action: climb the mountain. Don't just read the manuals at the bottom of base camp, but find that Sherpa.

Moneeka: Nice, because your Sherpa will make it more blissful.

Mark: They will definitely make it more blissful.

Moneeka: Okay. And tell us one strategy to being successful in real estate investing.

Mark: I think a strategy to being successful in real estate investing is about your internal metric. And that is to enjoy the process of meeting your goals. So, however you define success, I think that would be a strategy to get there, to really be crystal clear on what it is you want. I can't tell you how many people I talk to tell me they want to make $100 million in real estate. Well, like why? And by the fifth "why," it's really because they want to spend more time with their friends and family.

Well, you can get that without having $100 million. So let's talk about your idea of security, your idea of deepening relationships. I think it kind of needs to start more from (I hate to say it) a "choose your blissful strategy" than it is, "Yeah, let's just make a ton of money in real estate and let's implement this strategy." Because what's going to happen is exactly what we just discussed earlier, Moneeka; they're going to be sitting on their couch, reading your book, crying, saying, "You told me how to have this blissful experience and I ignored you and I chased this false sense of success."

Moneeka: Great. I love that. And so Mark, tell us one daily practice that you would say contributes to your success.

Mark: I have a gratitude journal, and every morning, I write in my gratitude journal. And of course, I have a system. So I start with the things that are a little bit below the surface of the things that I just am naturally grateful for. Like grateful for my wife, I'm grateful for my health, I'm grateful for my family. Those things are already checked off the list. But then it's like, I'm grateful for the fact that I don't have to call HR when I get sick. Or I'm grateful for the fact that I live in an area that only has a few cloudy days. I might be grateful for the flower that's growing in my front yard or that cool breeze on a Phoenix morning.

So these things, I want to go a little deeper, just the fact that I can wake up and think "How amazing is this?" Like I have clean water. Like there's parts of the world you've got to go to a river half a mile down, you've got to boil the water. I'm just waking up and I'm drinking water. I don't need to think about it.

These things I'm really trying to dig deeper down and feel very grateful for. Once I start my day like that, whatever happens out there really doesn't affect me as much.

Moneeka: I love that! I call gratitude the master skill of bliss. It works! Mark, you're awesome. I just want to say how incredibly nice this conversation has been, and I'm so grateful for the wisdom you've shared with my group, and just giving us a real tangible system and plan. I think it's really going to contribute to their toolbox. So thank you so much for being so generous with your time and your information.

Mark: Moneeka, thank you so much. In all seriousness, I'm honored and humbled to be on your podcast. Thank you.

*"To obtain financial freedom, one must be either
a business owner, an investor, or both, generating
passive income, particularly on a monthly basis."*
~ROBERT KIYOSAKI

HOW INTERNATIONAL INVESTORS CAN BUILD WEALTH IN AMERICAN REAL ESTATE
WITH FRANCOIS BRAINE-BONNAIRE

Moneeka: Today I'd like to welcome our guest Francois Braine-Bonnaire. Francois is a true Parisian who fell in love with the United States after interning in Los Angeles and New York during his business school years in France. Real estate in France had always intrigued him, but it is very pricey there, there is no rental yield, and the legal system badly favors tenants over landlords. So, in 2010 he moved to the United States. Francois's story is fascinating, and I'd love to have him share it.

Hello, Francois, welcome to the show.

Francois: Hello, Moneeka, so glad to be with you.

Moneeka: Francois, please share with us your story of how you came to the U.S. I lived in France for a time, and the story of people moving to different countries is always intriguing to me.

Francois: Thank you so much. Indeed I'm a native of Paris and I have a dual citizenship, French and American. I'm 45 years old, and like you, Moneeka, I've always enjoyed traveling around the world.

Attending business school in France gave me the opportunity to discover the United States when I interned in Los Angeles and New York.

After business school, I became an entrepreneur and co-founded an advertising agency in Paris back in 2000. Advertising is a difficult industry, and advertisers aren't always very loyal clients. In 2010, I was getting a bit tired of that and I was fascinated by the US, so I was ready to cross the big pond.

At the same time, there was a big economic meltdown in the US with this huge housing crisis. It was very sad, but it was also an exciting opportunity.

I decided to move to the US to start a brand new career in real estate investments. I had some cash funds to invest because I had sold my shares of the French co-founded advertising agency. I was ready to go and I came here with a blank sheet but willing to become a real estate investor myself.

When I got here, many people were speaking about Florida, Georgia, and also a little bit about Alabama. I started to invest myself and to buy single-family houses in these states that I was going to hold as rentals. Like you, Moneeka, I love passive income, so I progressively built my portfolio of single-family homes. And I have been actually living from the net rents since 2012. It is great; it gives me freedom.

Along with that, I started a website called USA-IMMO.COM in order to make people from around the globe aware that they have this kind of opportunity. They can invest in real estate here, even if they are non-US residents. And if they invest wisely, with my help they can enjoy the same kind of income.

In the past years, I was able to help more than 200 families in 15 different countries. France as a country has been very important in my real estate business here in the US, as French people love to save money. They are very different from Americans on that, and as they are big savers, they have a lot of cash to invest. I have helped people acquire about 600 rental properties that they hold as rentals while enjoying the passive income. And after several years they resell their properties that often have very nice appreciation, so they are very happy investors.

Moneeka: Nice. Where exactly do you live?

Francois: When I first moved to the US in 2010, I lived in Washington, DC for a while, which is a very expensive city. I was traveling all the time until I moved to Tampa, Florida, which was really the first market I invested in. At the time, Florida was badly stricken by foreclosures, but it was an amazing market to work with as an investor.

And then that market became very expensive again as Florida was one of the first states to bounce back, property values-wise. In 2015, I moved to

Birmingham, Alabama, which is a city that I love, too. Most French people would not be able to put Alabama on a map. I fell in love with the city. For your audience, Birmingham is definitely a good place to visit, and it's still not very well known.

Moneeka: Awesome. I'm curious to know why you decided to invest in Florida, Alabama, and Georgia. You have lived in two of the states, but how did you decide to start investing in Georgia, too?

Francois: I was trying to be involved in cities of different sizes. Atlanta is like the capital of the South: it's a huge city and has the biggest airport in the world. Birmingham is smaller, we're talking about a million people metro, compared to five million people in Atlanta. I was willing to be invested in different cities as I didn't want to put all my eggs in the same basket. There was also a convenience factor because it was an easy one-hour flight to travel from one city to another as the three states are next to each other.

Moneeka: Nice. This is actually an interesting piece because I tend to invest closer to where I live so I can have my thumb on the heartbeat of a market and I know how things work.

I feel more comfortable investing that way, so it's very interesting to hear that you did a similar thing. You moved to Florida and then to Alabama and invested in both areas. But it's not necessary to do that if you know experts locally like yourself whose expertise you can take advantage of.

Francois: That is absolutely true; I really want to rely on other people's expertise. For example, I don't manage my properties myself. The property managers I've selected charge me 10% of the collected rents, and I think that's the best investment I can make because it saves so much time. I use local expertise to manage my properties.

Moneeka: Awesome. I am curious about property management and would like you to talk more about it, but first, tell me about your best memory in real estate.

Francois: My best memory in real estate was initiated in 2011 when I had a real estate mentor in Tampa, Florida, who by the way is still a mentor and a friend.

This person told me I should buy a specific house, and to be honest, I was not excited at all about that house because it was a very small, old construction, bungalow-style wood-frame house. In Florida, that's not the best piece of property in my opinion, but I said okay and I bought it.

All in, I invested just $50,000, including the renovation, for a house with three bedrooms, located in a promising up and coming area of Tampa.

In 2017, I sold it and netted $143,000 for it. And during the rental years between purchase and sale, this house brought me $38,000 in net income.

It was just the best possible recipe for an investor: yield plus appreciation.

For me, the good lesson to learn is that you should have mentors and you need to commit to start. So surround yourself with experts or mentors, and just do it!

Moneeka: Something that international investors who are listening to the show might be considering is how to choose a mentor to help them to invest in the United States. One of the things that I always advise people is when you are picking a mentor, to pick someone who has also had rough times, not people that have had an easy ride, because there is no such thing as a business that does not have challenges. And we have challenges in real estate, too! But if you have the tools to be blissful and if you have a mentor who has been through the cycles, they can help you get through the tough times much more easily. Could you share with us your worst memory in real estate?

Francois: Absolutely. And you're right: real estate investment can seem a little bit scary. But if you know what to expect and if you are well advised, ultimately it is the best investment, much better and more reliable than the stock market.

One very bad memory for me is when I had to have one of my tenants evicted because she was not going to pay rent. It was very painful dealing with her.

Right after the eviction, the ex-tenant came back to the house with the goal of damaging and vandalizing it. She managed to do that after eviction but just before the property manager was able to secure the house, and she caused a lot of damage. I was upset because there were a lot of costly repairs needed. But fortunately, I had good insurance. I really consider insurance to be a key to success, so I've never been cheap on paying that cost and I always try to get top-notch coverage. The insurance pay-out was more than the amount of money actually needed to fix the house! There wasn't a cash flow issue because the house was quickly repaired, and I got a better tenant. So, I was able to quickly forget about this headache.

Lesson learned? As we say in France, you can't make an omelette without breaking eggs. The bottom line is: when something is very important, like insurance, do not be cheap. Get yourself the best coverage even if it costs you more money. Because when you need it, you are going to appreciate that you have it.

Moneeka: So tell me a little bit about insurance. Could you give us some tips on what you look for and what kind of coverage you are interested in?

Francois: Insurance is a complicated topic that I have studied carefully during my initial years, so I really understand it well now. There are two kinds of coverages: DP1, or the better and more comprehensive one, DP3.

And then you must also consider what kind of payment are you going to receive in case of a large claim? Is it going to be based on replacement cost or is it going to be based on actual cash value? If it's actual cash value, be careful because the insurance is going to use depreciation against you.

So let's say you buy a rental property for $100,000, and you have been holding it for five years. The insurance company will say it's not going to be worth $100,000 because there is depreciation, so they are going to refund you just a percentage of what you paid for. That's very dangerous, so replacement cost is always the best.

This is how replacement cost works: if your property is badly damaged, the insurance company will estimate the amount of money to pay you on the basis of how much it costs to rebuild the property as it was before the damage.

And finally, consider the deductible. You can have it as low as $1,000 deductible per claim on a rental; or you can have higher deductibles for cheaper insurance premiums. Low deductible has my preference.

Moneeka: Got it. I love that! Nobody has ever told me about that, so that's awesome. So tell me who are your best clients?

Francois: My clients are from around the world,
People who obviously have trust in the US economy.
People who are aware that real estate investment is the best investment possible because of its steady and high returns.
People who have cash to invest. Because if you are not a US resident, unfortunately it's going to be pretty much impossible to borrow money here, or in the foreign country where you live, in order to buy a piece property in the US.
Also, they are interested in having property that generates positive cash flow. Abroad, in Europe for example, if you are trying to buy a rental property in London or in Paris, there is no yield; you are just betting on appreciation, but there is close to zero yield after taxes.

Those are my good clients.

And they all value my expertise because they know that I've put a lot of my own personal money in the same kinds of rental properties I'm going to help them buy.

Moneeka: Nice. What is it that you offer your clients that others don't? What makes you different?

Francois: To sum it up, you can say that I comprehensively help non-US residents invest successfully in US residential real estate for passive income.

I'm confident to state that I might be the most thorough and reliable person that you will ever do business with.

I'm delivering to my clients, on a silver platter, everything they need to invest here:

-the real estate turnkey providers, as you can't do everything yourself from abroad. You need someone to buy, rehab, and manage the properties and tenants for you.

But also I'll provide them, as needed, with:

-top-notch real estate attorneys to close the acquisitions safely and properly.

-CPA for taxes in the USA to be well handled and optimized.

-and, as mentioned, insurance expertise.

And last but not least, I'm sharing with my clients my own and very significant experience as a landlord.

Moneeka: Got it! I love that you cover so much because you have a sensitivity to what it's like to be an international person investing in the US.

In the United States, there are a lot of laws and rules. Because we live here, we take for granted that we know about them and we have a consciousness around how to deal with them. But when you bring money from abroad, to a completely different country, it's hard to know all of those details. It's absolutely amazing what you are providing!

Could you talk a little bit about property management and how that works for you and your investors? For instance, if something were to go wrong with the property manager, do you help the investor find a new one? Have you dealt with that situation in the past?

Francois: That's a very good question, and I have actually had to deal with this one time in the past. One property manager was no longer performing well, and it was necessary to find a new one. The good thing is that

I'm in the same boat as my clients, as since 2012 I've been making my living off the net collected rents. So when something is not working, I'm the first person to be concerned and willing to fix it.

So in that situation mentioned, I found an alternative property management company, and then I tested it myself on my own houses. After doing so successfully I said to my clients, "If you think that the property manager is not performing the way they used to, I've got someone else I've tested, that you can move to." So bottom line, yes, I'm there to help them long-term because I'm invested myself.

I'm not basically selling turnkey rental properties; but I'm a seasoned investor, sharing my knowledge.

Moneeka: Wow! I love that.

Francois: Property management is a cornerstone for the success of your real estate investment. They are doing a lot for their clients.

For example, if someone all of a sudden no longer pays the rent, you will have to evict this person. How will you manage an eviction if you live in Paris? You are not going to do it yourself. The property manager, who knows the procedure, will take care of everything for you, keep you updated, and make sure the process is completed swiftly and at lowest costs.

In the United States, an eviction process can take less than 60 days, but in Paris if you want to evict someone, it can take 18 months! Yes, it's a nightmare.

Moneeka: Wow! That is truly awesome. I'm very impressed with how you take care of your clients.

Francois, I wanted to ask you about what's next for you. I know you've got some exciting things coming up.

Francois: Thank you for asking.

I've recently become a certified life coach.

So as of 2020, I'll offer my services, with focuses on:

-entrepreneurship and conducting international affairs, on the business side,

-and balancing your life well, on the personal side.

I'm going to partner on that with my life partner, Maegan, who has a PhD in counselling.

All that being said, real estate investments & passive income will always be one of my main activities.

Moneeka: That's awesome; thank you for sharing that with us! Tell us how people can get in touch with you.

Francois: The best way would be through e-mail and I'm always extremely responsive to that. My email is francois@usa-immo.com. People can expect, even when I'm traveling, to get an answer from me within 24 hours.

Moneeka: Perfect. Is there a free gift you want to offer my audience?

Francois: Yes, absolutely! Thank you for the opportunity. For people who feel that they are seriously interested in those good turnkey real estate investments in the US—and especially for your audience abroad, Moneeka—I'll be happy to offer a free 20-minute one-on-one consultation. Just contact me by e-mail and we will schedule that.

Moneeka: Thank you; that is so generous and so useful.
Now it's time for our three rapid-fire questions, Francois.
Can you give us one super tip on getting started in real estate investing?

Francois: Real estate is not risky. You are buying an asset and if you are not satisfied with it down the road, you can resell it. You just have to avoid certain mistakes. For example, never buy property in a badly distressed residential area. So as the risk is really manageable, just start and do it: become a real estate investor!

Moneeka: Nice. Can you tell us one strategy on being successful in real estate investing?

Francois: That comes back to surrounding yourself with people who have expertise and who have a successful track record.
Moneeka, you are one of those, and I trust I am, too.
Find a win/win deal with them, like the one I offer to my clients: I charge no (0) fees to them for my comprehensive help, but I'm compensated by the real estate properties' sellers.

Moneeka: Nice! Finally, can you tell us a daily practice, Francois, that contributes to your personal success?

Francois: Business-wise, at the end of each day I take a few minutes to do a small recap, to sort the good stuff of the day and the not good stuff and try to think about how to improve on them next time.

On the personal side: balancing your life well. Work and finance are important, but so are well-being and fitness to get rid of stress. And needless to say: spend quality time with your loved ones.

And beside those daily practices, regularly travelling and discovering different cultures and countries is very important in my life, I keep on learning so much from it.

Moneeka: My husband and I have a true passion for travel. We've been married 25 years and have visited over 55 countries together, so you can tell we spend a lot of time on the road and it's really awesome.

Francois: That's really impressive! Congratulations for being married for 25 years, and for having visited 55 countries together.

Moneeka: Thank you! Francois, this has been so much fun and so informative; thank you so much for sharing all of your wisdom with my audience.

Francois: Thank you very much. I was very happy to be on the show today. Thank you, Moneeka, for the opportunity.

> *"You can't make an omelet without breaking eggs*
> *. . . so don't be afraid to break eggs. Keep on being*
> *dedicated and thorough, and it will pay off."*
> ~FRANCOIS BRAINE-BONNAIRE

Savvy Tips to Ensure Your Success

Here are additional skills to help you create the success your heart deeply desire.

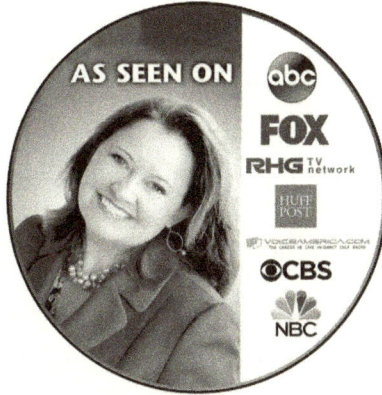

THE MAGIC OF MANAGING TIME ON PURPOSE
WITH REBECCA HALL GRUYTER

Moneeka: Today, I would like to welcome to the show our amazing guest, Rebecca Hall Gruyter.

Rebecca Hall Gruyter (CEO of Your Purpose Driven Practice and RHG Media Productions™) specializes in highlighting experts to help them reach more people around the world! From the Speaker Talent Search™ (that helps you find more speaking opportunities), podcast opportunities (syndicated on multiple networks), to writing opportunities including . . . bringing your book forward as a bestseller.

She is an award-winning #1 international bestselling author multiple times over . . . published in over five magazines and over 20 books. A popular talk radio show host/producer, dynamic TV show host/producer, creator of the Women's Empowerment Conference Series, and an in-demand guest expert and speaker.

Rebecca has been recognized by CBS, ABC, Fox, and NBC as a Top Professional in the area of Purpose Driven Entrepreneurship. With a promotional reach of over 10 million, she is committed to helping you reach more people around the world as you step into a place of influence! Remember, what the world needs is more of YOU!

I invited Rebecca to the show because she is insanely good at managing time and creating success in all areas of her life. Rebecca is involved in lots of projects, and to do that, she has mastered the art of time management and getting things done.

When I'm out and about talking to people about real estate, one of the biggest objections they have about getting started in investing is that they don't have the time, which I totally understand. That is exactly why I wanted to have this conversation with Rebecca because if anybody can talk to us about time management and getting the things done in our life that we want to get done, she is our lady.

On that note, welcome to the show, Rebecca. How are you?

Rebecca: I'm good, thank you. My goodness! What a great introduction.

Moneeka: It's all true. You amaze me.

Rebecca, you have so much going on in your life; do people ask you all the time, "When do you sleep? Do you see your husband ever?" Tell us a little bit about how this works in your life.

Rebecca: Absolutely, and it is something I get asked all the time. When you asked me to be on the show, I really sank into this question and I thought, what is it? How do I do all these different things, and how can I help others figure out their formula for success? Because I don't believe it's really going to help you or any of your listeners to know exactly what I do in a day and how I do it. But I want to really help each of you do it your way so that you can shine and really step forward in a powerful way.

I think the reason I get asked that question a lot is because I'm very result-oriented, and I'm launching programs and releasing projects on a fairly regular basis. Frequently, people don't understand that there were many little steps that took place behind the scenes before they see the final product. It didn't just all happen in one day; it really was step by step by step. Then we announce it, and finally we bring it forward.

I think if we can learn to break tasks down, step by step by step, we are all going to be highly productive and keep launching products or projects and have people ask us that very same question.

And I do see my husband, by the way! In fact, today is date night, and I'm getting off early. We'll go out and have a great time, even though it's the middle of the week. We purposely carve that time out.

Moneeka: Thank you so much for mentioning all of those things. I think a lot of people—when they are looking at investing in real estate or investing in any kind of business—are excited about that end result. They want to have the house, have the business, have the success, have the money, and they have seen people that have done it. What we need to remember is that the people we see who are successful now were not out there shining at the very beginning; they are out there shining now because they have results, but there was so much that happened before to get them there.

Rebecca: Yes.

Moneeka: And so many times we forget that there were all those other little steps. Now, it doesn't mean that all those other things have to be over-whelming, but they still do need to happen. Writing them down, staying focused on each result and on each step along the way, is really helpful to get us to that place that we want to get to. Unfortunately, we don't get to start at the end!

Rebecca: No magic wand!

Moneeka: I wish there was, but we don't get to start at the end. We have to start at the beginning.

Rebecca: Exactly.

Moneeka: Tell us a little bit more about that. How do you successfully move so many things forward?

Rebecca: As I was preparing for today, I remembered my parents play-ing a song for me—or maybe it was a nursery rhyme—that said:

"Inch by inch, life's a cinch; yard by yard, life's hard."
[Originally a quote by John Bytheway]

Sometimes I find we are trying to take yard-long steps instead of little inch-by-inch or millimeters or centimeters, but those little inches still add up to the yard. They still add up to where we are going. When we become overwhelmed or we get stuck, and moving forward feels really hard, it's because we are trying to take a yard-long step. All we need to do is take an inch today, an inch tomorrow, and an inch the next day.

It is almost like when we were in school and we had different subjects. This is the math hour, then we have recess and move around, and then we go to history. We move around a little bit, and then we go to this class or that class. Now, if we can break up our day like that, into these little seg-ments where we are focused on this piece and we honor that, we move around a little bit, and then we go to the next and the next, we are moving forward in all of those areas every single day.

Moneeka: Rebecca, I love that! Can you break it down a little bit more, like in a business day?

Rebecca: Sure. I have different projects that I am working on right now. I have two anthologies I'm leading with multiple authors. We just released our new magazine—we are in the promotional phase of that—and we have already started the next ones so they will be ready for release next quarter.

We are holding a conference in three weeks, which we are still promoting and getting logistical pieces in place; we are also doing a stealth launch of our private book projects. Off the top of my head, those are just a few of the projects that we are working on.

If I were to structure today, for example, I had to allow time for a class I was teaching for an Arizona-based leadership team earlier this morning; I had to allow time for the show that we are doing now; I will work on the anthologies for a half hour or an hour; I have a communication hour because those e-mails and Facebook and other social media need attention; I will have an hour to work on promotional projects; and then I have meetings.

So that's some of what's taking place today, and I'm still getting off early to spend time with my husband! Notice that I have broken down the day into smaller steps instead of "I'm going to finish the whole book" or "I'm going to finish the whole anthology." I've broken each project into steps we can take today. I'm a little bit of an overachiever, people say sometimes . . .

Moneeka: I wouldn't really say that about you! (teasing)

Rebecca: How I interpret that to mean is that I like extra credit. I like to do more, above and beyond what I said I was going to do; that's exciting to me. So, every day, I will make a list of priorities: A, B, and C. The A priorities are absolutely committed: this is my time to devote to this project. For example, my time with you is nonnegotiable; we are doing the show today. I had that training earlier today. So those are on my A list, but then I have my B list. My C list is the extra credit items I could do. And one of those C-list items was to call my husband and see if we could get together early today and I did that, so I got extra credit. I'm already ahead!

By first breaking your day or projects down into those smaller pieces, you will know that if the step feels hard and heavy, and you have been staring at that same paper for a half hour, it's a yard-long step. It's too big. You need to break it down into a smaller piece, into a step that you can take. And maybe the step is to reevaluate the project, to break it down even further, because sometimes we try to take too big a step and that can stop us or get us stuck.

Moneeka: That's really interesting. Even I get stuck in this. I, like you, really like my lists and so I have this long to-do list of tasks that I want to get done by the end of the day. And I am, like you, an overachiever, and so my list is really long. What happens for me is that at the end of the day, when I have only finished half of the tasks on the list, I feel bad and overwhelmed that there are all these items still left, that they didn't get done.

And I love the idea of prioritizing: these are my A-list tasks and this is my B list and this is my C list. And if the B list doesn't get done, it's okay because the B list will become part of the A list eventually, and I don't need to feel bad about that. What wears me out is not feeling successful at the end of the day. Instead, I feel overwhelmed. I think, "Oh gosh, I didn't get it all done and I'm already behind before tomorrow morning." Would you agree with that?

Rebecca: Absolutely, and you can reevaluate during the day. I actually did that during lunch. I looked at the list for today and I reevaluated. How am I doing on the list? Do I need to reprioritize anything? What can I cross off? And I don't let myself add tasks on!

Moneeka: Oh, that's interesting!

Rebecca: You don't get to add tasks halfway through the day unless you take something off the A list and move it to the B or C list. Because here's the deal, and this is what is really powerful and exciting about time:

We all get the same amount. It's a fair giver: every day we get 24 hours and we get to choose how it's spent. We get to choose! How often in our life do we give ourselves permission to do that? I'm going to spend my time here, I'm going to spend my time there—we can do that every single day. So, halfway through the day, I check in with how I have been spending my time. Do I want to spend it differently looking toward the remaining time I have left today?

Moneeka: Interesting.

Rebecca: What do I want to shuffle around? And part of where we get lost around time is that we get muddled. We put tasks on our list with no time allotted to it; it's just a task on our list. And it could be a 10-minute task, it could be a 30-minute task, it could be a five-hour task, but we give it the same weight as all the other tasks on our list.

I look at time as a 24-hour plate. We need to sleep, we want to shower, to shave, to get ready, do things like that. In the same 24 hours, we need to eat. We can't forget to add in time for transportation.

We sometimes forget about that transportation piece. We think we are teleporting. We don't allow time to . . . drive, we don't allow time to eat, we don't allow time to pause and breathe. In fact, allowing time to pause and breathe helps you go faster because you can check in and choose how you spend your next minute on purpose rather than just going to the next thing.

I believe we should reevaluate throughout the day whatever we are doing because we get hijacked. We are hijacked when we become distracted by something that will run away with us. We suddenly look up and our time is gone, and we didn't get the tasks on our list done because we got hijacked.

And remember to expect to have unexpected things happen. If we look back on every previous 24 hours we have ever had, there have been surprises. There has been an unexpected call, something has taken longer than we expected, we have had e-mails come up, or something urgent that we need to address; every 24 hours that happens. If we know that, let's build that in, and if it doesn't happen, guess what? We can go to our B list and C list and get ahead.

Moneeka: Yay!

Rebecca: By committing to a fewer number of tasks on the A list, we are setting ourselves up for success. And really scrutinize the A list when you are creating it; look at how long those tasks take and when you are choosing to do them. Are you actually putting them in the calendar or just hoping it all gets done by the end of the day? Because you can't keep pushing the tasks off by thinking, "I'll start that in five minutes" or "I'll get to that later." So those are ways that you can start to take control and have time work for you.

Another strategy you can use is to touch something only one time instead of putting it on a to-do list. And this can be really sneaky because what we usually do is look at something—we will read that email or we will receive something—and we think, "I'll deal with that later." Then we spend time building a later list, and then we become overwhelmed because we haven't moved forward with our priority list. Whereas if we allowed a little bit of cushion in the day, we could take care of those small tasks one time, in three minutes or less, and it's done; it never, ever has to go on your to-do list. You will have finished all of those extra, one-time items along with your priority A list during the day. I can give you an example if you want.

Moneeka: Yes, I would love that.

Rebecca: I get anywhere from 500 to 1,000 e-mails a day—that's just e-mail, that's not all the social media communication—plus everything else that I'm doing in a day because I'm not just sitting in front of the computer waiting for e-mails.

Moneeka: That is the same for me.

Rebecca: I choose to check e-mail in the morning—although I do check it a few times during the day—and I delete the ones that I don't need to deal with or they are not relevant to what is going on right now. I check my A, B, and C lists, and I only open the e-mail that I am ready to spend one to three minutes on and deal with.

If I open it up and it's an invitation to something that I know is no, I respond and say no. If it's thank you very much, I received that, I will spend the few minutes filing the e-mail or doing whatever I need to do to track it in our system.

When I have the chapters coming in from the different authors, I open the e-mail. I acknowledge it, letting the author know I received it and when they will hear back from me. I go into my systems and spreadsheets to document everything, and then I file it in the appropriate way so it's ready for the next step. That takes three minutes: it's done, and the task never has to go on my list, and I never have to spend a full day just working on author acknowledgements.

And if I take these 15 minutes or 30 minutes that I have built into my day for communication, it never has to become an overwhelming task on my to-do list.

And something else happened this morning. After the class I taught this morning, I took a break to move around a little bit because it's important to move, not just stay in one place all the time. I went outside and looked at the garden; I noticed that it was getting a little crazy out there and snails were attacking my kale! I recalled seeing a video on YouTube about putting Coca-Cola in a spray bottle and spraying the plants with it—then the bugs and snails won't attack the plants anymore—so I thought I'm going to go find a spray bottle.

I spent about five minutes looking for the spray bottle, but I couldn't find it. I stopped and decided that since this was going to be more than a five-minute activity, I would put it on my list and ask my husband because he might actually know where to find the spray bottle. We don't have to do everything ourselves! When he comes home, I'll ask him. I might have a result in a minute or I will need to put on my list to find the spray bottle and spray the plants. Did you see how I stopped myself and I didn't get lost spending 15 or 30 minutes on this shiny object?

Moneeka: Right.

Rebecca: But it is still important to me. Here is the step I can take—ask my husband—and then I move back into focus, back to the tasks that I want to move forward on today.

Moneeka: I think what is really interesting about this is that the "shiny objects syndrome" is so easy to get caught in. Many of the people who are listening to the show are entrepreneurs, are professional women, and they have full time jobs and they are thinking about investing in real estate on the side. I teach a workshop on identifying the steps to get to success, and each of those steps then has steps within them. But you sit down to do that one step and then you think, "I need to do laundry" or "I should clean the kitchen" or what you were talking about with the snails outside.

Rebecca: I've got to protect my kale!

Moneeka: Right, and it is true: all of these things are important. But really designating time for the project, that's important, too, and that time should be sacred. Yes, set time aside for when you need to do the laundry, for when you go grocery shopping, to do all of those things that we have to do to make life run, but don't allow them to interfere with your project time.

Rebecca: Yes.

Moneeka: Even if you only give yourself a half hour for that project, allow yourself to fully focus for that half hour because that is the thing that is going to get you, inch by inch, to success. We don't have to do a huge amount to experience success, but we do consistently have to do those little inches, right?

Rebecca: Absolutely! I'm resonating so much with what you're saying. I was a financial advisor, working with organizations and companies, when I started this women's empowerment project as a hobby that grew and evolved to become a business, so I got to make a choice. I absolutely understand what it is like to live in multiple worlds, to be fully serving in the role that you have and to be building toward your future on the side as well. It is absolutely doable, but it takes that discipline and it takes that focus and that commitment, inch by inch.

Moneeka: Yes! Rebecca, tell us, what is the "full plate syndrome"?

Rebecca: Think of 24 hours like a dinner plate, and you are going to fill it. If you have been to buffets or potlucks where everybody brings wonderful food and you don't quite know what's at the other end of the table where you start—and they always start with the vegetables. I like vegetables, don't get me wrong, but I love chocolate cake, and I know there is something chocolate somewhere on the table!

As I'm building my plate, I say yes to this and that and I'm going to try this or that. Then I start to get more and more careful as I go down the table because I see my plate filling up. Each spot on my plate becomes a little bit more precious, and suddenly there is a cucumber rolling off, maybe an olive, but I'm okay with that because now I have room for chocolate cake! When I reach the end of the table and look up, I see that there is another table with food that I hadn't planned for, and yet my plate is full.

Moneeka: Oh!

Rebecca: What we do is we keep adding items; very rarely do I see anyone at these potlucks scooping something off the plate to make room for the chocolate cake. And yet we can do that. If we keep adding things on to our plate, there is a point where it's full. You can't fit more in the 24 hours. This is it, so we have to reevaluate.

Moneeka: Right.

Rebecca: That's the full plate syndrome: you just keep piling things on. I love saying yes, but sometimes saying yes can also mean saying no to something else you may not even know about because you don't always know what's coming. It is really important to guard what you put on your plate, what you let others put on your plate, and what you say yes to; you should put on your plate only what really matters to you.

If you keep adding tasks and something comes up you didn't expect and, oh my goodness, this is the thing that could change your life or this is something you need to do or be a part of, then you have got to see what you can take off your plate to make room for the new opportunity.

Moneeka: Got it. So, what is the most effective way you would manage that?

Rebecca: If I have people in the classroom—and they get a little bit feisty about this—I put a big circle on the wall and this is their plate. I have them take big sticky notes where they list everything that they are doing, and they list and they list, and sticky notes are on top of sticky notes are on top of sticky notes. I ask them to start assigning times. This is when they get a little irritated because they now have to go back through all the sticky notes and assign times.

I then ask, "Did you remember eating, sleeping, transportation?" They roll their eyes and get a little more frustrated, and they add those, too. Then they start adding up the time and see that they are trying to do 40 hours of tasks in 24 hours. No wonder they are not getting it all done; no wonder they are feeling frazzled and spread too thin and that they don't have time for themselves. Because we each only have 24 hours.

This shows that you need to break some of those tasks down in smaller pieces, you need to move them out, you need to perhaps say no to some things, delegate some things, take some things off. You have 24 hours: that is the container, that is the space, and that is where you need to start. You need to really look at where you are at, and then you can make decisions about right sizing. And then there is time for extra credit opportunities. Being the overachiever I am, I love that.

Here is the challenge: try NOT to fully fill your 24 hours. Leave an opening on your plate for the chocolate cake you don't know about, live in anticipation of that new thing, or an opportunity that is waiting for you. Create the space so you can take advantage of an unexpected opportunity. Then you don't have to take something off your plate to fit it in.

We don't have any problem filling space. We are going to do something on our extra credit list anyway, so give yourself space for what is to come.

Moneeka: Hmm, I love that. The other idea that I really love is when you talked about date night, which is something I have implemented in my life. I have been married for over 25 years, and every single week for all those years, we have had a date night. And in those times where I am working 16 hours a day—that doesn't happen for very long because I don't want to burn out; I want real estate investing to stay joyful, to be my passion—I still have date night with my husband. And that is the reward for everything that I do during the week, like the light at the end of the tunnel.

And I think it is really important that as we plan for all those to-dos that we talk about and plan for the chocolate cake. It is not just something else that we want; it is also a reward that we have to allow for in our time so that all the things that we are doing feel worthwhile. Wouldn't you agree?

Rebecca: Exactly! We can squeeze the life out of our life if we are not careful. It can get buried in the to-do list, as if we are saving the reward for someday—I'll get to do this someday. Instead, we can actually build the reward into how we spend our time and our energy today.

Moneeka: Awesome! Unfortunately, we are running out of time. Do you have any final advice or tips for my listeners before we move into our rapid-fire questions?

Rebecca: Just a reminder that you are precious. Each of you is absolutely needed and the gift of who you are and how you spend your time and your energy really matters. It is not something to push to the side, and I want to encourage each of you to purposely choose to spend it in ways that matter to you. This will help make your life and the world a better place because when you are choosing on purpose, you are living on purpose. And you are bringing forward those things that matter to you and that is how we make a positive impact.

Moneeka: Thank you. That is such valuable advice.
Rebecca, before we go into our rapid-fire questions, how can people reach you?

Rebecca: The easiest way to reach me is through my website, <u>YourPurposeDrivenPractice.com</u>, where there is a contact form.
What I would like to do for your listeners today is to make myself available. If any of you want to explore time, look at what is on that plate, and get support around how you can play to your strengths, let's chat. I want to make sure that what you are doing is done in a way where you shine. Not by doing it someone else's way, but your way. I would love to have a conversation about that and give you some ideas. You can schedule a time at **Error! Hyperlink reference not valid.**, and we will set up a 30-minute conversation.

Moneeka: Wow! Thank you. That is the free gift everybody. Just to be really clear: Rebecca is very generously offering some of her time to talk specifically about how you can manage your time. Thank you so much, Rebecca; that was very generous.

Rebecca: My pleasure.

Moneeka: Great! Are you ready for our three rapid-fire questions?

Rebecca: Ready!

Moneeka: Rebecca, tell us one super tip on getting started in investing in real estate.

Rebecca: Generally, if you are looking to start a business, you want to have a plan. You want to look at your idea and what you want to accomplish with it. You need to have a direction, from how you want to start the business to where you want the business to go. And this plan needs to be specific: what do you want, what will it look like, what will it feel like, how will it grow, how will you measure that you have arrived there? And remember that you can get support. You don't have to do this on your own; it is not a solo journey.

Moneeka: Awesome, thank you for that. Tell us one strategy on being successful in real estate investing.

Rebecca: A lot of it is a mindset. One of the things that we need to do is to take steps, like you were talking about earlier. Step by step by step and broken down into the little inches so we can take the steps.

Also, remember that when we tell ourselves "I have to" or "I should," that those are very disempowering, heavy ways to be. Instead, if we can catch ourselves and say "I choose," "I will," or "I am," our mindset will be very different.

It is important to pay attention to what we say to ourselves and even what we say out loud! You might say to someone, "This is hard" or "I have so many things on my to-do list, I'll never get it all done," and your mind will agree!

Moneeka: You know that I am all about choice; my book is called Choose Bliss. Everything that we do is about choice. Even when we feel like it's not, it really is!

This is the last question, Rebecca. What is one daily practice that you would say contributes to your success?

Rebecca: Can I share two?

Moneeka: Of course. You are such an overachiever!

Rebecca: I love that extra credit, that gold star.

I start every day on purpose, so the day isn't just happening to me. I wake up with a new 24 hours, and I get to decide how to spend it. I tend to make that prioritized list of what I am going to do the night before, to get it out of me and let my subconscious support me. The next morning I take some time and look at the list with excitement.

What am I going to do today? What am I going to spend time on? What are the steps, the inches, that I am going to bring forward? I actually get excited about all the things that are going to get done today!

Moneeka: Oh! I love that.

Rebecca: You start the day on purpose and then have a plan for the day. This is where you are going, this is what you will be doing. You need to make sure the plan is right-sized, that it actually fits within the 24 hours.

The third practice—okay, I have a third—is to remember to pause, especially when you are feeling overwhelmed. Especially if you are feeling like that one more thing that can't happen, does happen. In that moment, you pause, you take a breath, and ask yourself a question. For example, I will ask myself, "Rebecca, are you being who you want to be? Stressed out, frazzled, frustrated, feeling brittle, that one more thing you never want?" The answer is clearly no. Not with judgment, not with criticism, but with awareness; no, I am not being who I want to be or how I want to be.

Then with my next breath, I say, "Choose to be who you want to be and how you want to be." It takes 30 seconds, a minute, and somehow that stopping, that focusing, that checking in makes the day looks different. I can make different decisions; I can reevaluate, like I did today at lunch.

Now that I have 12 hours left, I check in and make sure those are still the priorities, or do I need to move something around? That changed my life, remembering to pause. I was really good at pushing forward and doing that next thing and that next thing—ignoring my body, ignoring needing rest, ignoring any of the warning signs—and would just keep pushing, pushing, pushing. But when I learned to stop, to pause, and to check in, I then had the ability to make different choices and truly be who I want to be, even in those crazy moments, and move forward in a way that is in alignment.

Moneeka: Wow! I just love that! It is true that powerful women believe that it is expected of us to just keep pushing forward. Push through it, push through the tired, push through the resistance. "Push, push, push," that is what we were taught. Unfortunately, no one is built to just keep pushing, and we do perform better if we take care of ourselves. Let's not forget about that.

Coming from you, that is really amazing advice. With all that you get done, it is just so great to see that you take the time for you, too.

Rebecca: Absolutely, it is necessary.

Moneeka: It is necessary, otherwise we can't perform or when we are performing, we are just not doing it at our best. Thank you for mentioning that.

Rebecca: Absolutely, yes.

Moneeka: Rebecca, thank you so much for being on the show today and sharing all of your amazing wisdom with us.

> *"Remember your time and energy are precious. Therefore, spend it wisely on purpose and with great purpose."*
> ~REBECCA HALL GRUYTER

STRESS-FREE REMODELING FOR MAXIMUM PROFIT
WITH EMMA AURIEMMA-MCKAY

Moneeka: Today, I am so excited to introduce you to Emma Auriemma-McKay. Emma is the author of Stress-Free Remodeling and the creator of The Ultimate Home Remodeling Blueprint Program.

Emma is on a mission to help people live in a home which they love, are proud of, and inspires them to do their very best work in the world. Emma has over 25 years experience, is a graduate of the Rhode Island School of Design, and is a licensed architect and interior designer.

I invited Emma to the show because of her architectural and interior design expertise. When I buy a repossessed or distressed property, I want to remodel it to make it into a really inviting home for a tenant and then hold the property for a while.

With Emma's extensive experience, she can walk into a home and see what is possible. I know that, as investors, those possibilities are going to be a really big key for how much money we put into a project in order to reap the benefit. In other words, if we put in too much money, we won't recover our cost in our rental or sale. If we put in too little money, the property will not be as inviting for the kinds of tenants we want.

Emma, thank you so much for coming and being on the show.

Emma: I am so excited to be here, Moneeka. Thank you for inviting me.

Moneeka: My pleasure. Let's start by talking about insider secrets that will help you save money on your remodel.

Emma: The first big thing is not to do much custom work. Some things may already be in place, such as kitchen cabinets and lighting fixtures, so if you can use what is existing, don't tear it out!

There are many ways you can add to what is existing; there are simple ways of painting cabinets to update them and make them look brand new. There are techniques to stain cabinets so they are a darker color, or you can replace just the faces of the cabinets, not the whole thing.

Kitchens are such an important part of a home and a new countertop could really up the appeal for tenants or prospective homeowners looking for that perfect kitchen. Everyone wants stone or some kind of a monolithic hard surface. There are standard countertops that you can buy from Home Depot or similar stores without going into custom work.

Moneeka: Another really good tip that I have used is getting the right hardware for the cabinetry. Something that I see with other landlords is that they aren't concerned about the kitchen, but I will tell you from experience that I always remodel the kitchen. I don't care whether it is a rental or it is your own home, whether it is your dream home or your first home, there is something about a kitchen that says family.

Emma: Of course, the kitchen is the heart of the home. The little addition of nice hardware is almost like adding jewelry to give so much more sparkle. Those little inexpensive details can make a big difference.

Moneeka: That's right. Whether or not someone notices the kitchen, whether a woman walks in and says, "I love that kitchen" or "I hate that kitchen"—and this includes men, this is not just a woman thing, this is the whole family—when we walk into a house, we look at the kitchen and we make our first impressions.

Emma: Right.

Moneeka: It is so critical that if you do nothing else, at least make the kitchen look inviting. It doesn't have to be spectacular, but it needs to be inviting. It needs to bring images of the family having a meal together.

Emma: Exactly. And there are nice little touches you can do. Add a little eating nook if there is room or hang pendant lights over the eating area, and don't forget the flooring.

Another area where you can save money for rental properties, is having durable floors. Rather than install wood floors, you can do great inexpensive vinyl floors that looks exactly like handcrafted wood. And there is now porcelain tile that looks like wood floors and it is insanely durable. There are really great things you can use to make the kitchen look spectacular for a very good price.

Moneeka: Right, and you can get all that at Home Depot. Like you mentioned, you don't have to be a pro, you don't have to have a license and work with special places; you can do this at Home Depot! That is really great advice, thank you. Are there other areas we can save money?

Emma: The other big target for remodels is the bathroom. Tile and the tubs are usually not in great shape. There are refinishing methods that can quickly repair and update them. Not only does that save money but time. When you are remodeling for resale or renting, time is a very
important factor. You want to do things quickly.

Moneeka: Emma, tell us important remodeling mistakes to avoid.

Emma: One mistake is putting way too much money into remodeling, such as flooring, which we mentioned. There are a variety of price ranges, and while you don't have to use the best quality, there are some really good quality options. It is important to be conscious of the quality and warranties on the products you buy.

Open-flowing floor plans are very popular these days, but many of the older homes have each room segmented and you don't have a sense of a flow.

I remodeled some houses years ago when I started out, and I was doing it as if it would have been in my home. We removed walls and we had to put in costly structural support. It made a huge improvement but at a great cost. Be aware of where you plan these changes and what the implications can be. Definitely, have advice from an engineer.

On another project, we took a wall out that wasn't load-bearing to increase the size of a living room. That was so much easier, but permits are still required for this kind of work.

There are simpler ways to open spaces up without having to get into a lot of structural work and cost. If there is an opening from one room to another, most likely it can be widened a little more. If there is no connection between a kitchen and family room or dining room, an opening, such as a large pass-through, can be made in the wall. That is not a big construction project, but the visual connection, function, and the added light quality between the two rooms will really be enhanced. This will result in that sense of flow that is so desirable.

If it is an older home, you may have to upgrade electricity and the plumbing, and you will need to have permits; please, don't get into trouble! It is important to comply with the building codes.

I've mentioned permits here a couple of times. Don't make the mistake not to get them. Getting a permit also involves inspections by your building department. Even though it is a bit of a hassle, quite frankly, it protects you by ensuring that the items that were installed are the proper products and the installation was done correctly. You can incur hefty fines if you get caught doing work without getting permits.

Doors and windows can enhance rooms, making them appear more spacious. If there is little or no connection with the outdoors, especially from a kitchen or family room I would say it is a mistake not to add a door for access or nice windows to enjoy a sense of openness. Your contractor can be a good source for good performing products at good prices.

Another area to avoid making a mistake is with paint color. Be conscious about what colors you use in the house because color can turn people off. Color is an important aspect of your interiors and decorating—how a home feels—but don't use wild colors. It is interesting because this year the popular color is violet. I don't know if many people realistically would be comfortable living with violet walls. A color like this can deter people from renting or buying the home. It's amazing how people cannot see beyond things like this. So I advise keeping the interior colors neutral. You can do accent walls with a warmer or darker tone than the other walls, but don't go too vibrant on colors. Keeping neutral colors but with variation in hue and using textures can still make a stunning impact.

I recently watched a home show where the remodelers who were flipping the house put periwinkle tile in the master bathroom and kitchen. To me, that was a little bit of risk.

Moneeka: Well, that color is better for a homeowner's personal house.

Emma: Right. Luckily for the flippers, they were doing this project in a beach town, and the prospective buyers did like it and the house sold quickly. But a word of caution: be aware of your market.

Moneeka: Neutral does not need to be boring: there are 50 different whites you can pick from!

Emma: Exactly!

Moneeka: What we might call renter's white is just a plain flat white, so I will usually pick a warmer white. Depending on the house and how the light is hitting it, I might have a yellow undertone or a pink undertone to give it a warmer feel but it still stays neutral.

And I love the accent wall idea. I usually let my tenants paint an accent wall to bring their colors into the home; then we repaint so the new tenants can do the same thing. Although colors can feel boring, there are a lot more options than you think.

Emma: Lastly, I also want to mention that making the house have show-stopper curb appeal is really important. It's a mistake not to invest a little to make the home inviting and it takes doing very simple things. A few of those simple things include changing out the front door or making it look really nice, and cleaning up the garage doors or even replacing them. Clean up and trim overgrown plants and maybe add a few strategically placed flowers. These few items can increase the price of a property and make it eye-catching for renters. They will feel at home, it is welcoming, and they will be happy to invite their friends to visit.

Moneeka: Yes, that is right. It really does increase the value price-wise, whether you are selling or you are renting. I have seen a dramatic shift in the price happen because of the curb appeal.

Emma: Isn't that amazing? Just simple things like that.

Moneeka: Yes! I might have the front door repainted and I will hang a wreath when people come and see the property; just doing little things like that will warm it up.

Emma: Yes.

Moneeka: Emma, we are already out of time, if you can believe it.

Emma: Oh, that was fast. There is always so much to say!

Moneeka: I wanted you to talk more about flow when taking down walls, but we don't have the time! Can you tell my listeners how they can get in touch with you?

Emma: They can get in touch with me at my website, StressFreeRemodeling.com or email me at Emma@StressFreeRemodeling.com. If it's okay,

Moneeka, I would like to offer a free gift I created. It is the Home Remodel Checklist: 5 Easy Steps to Start Your Remodel on the Right Foot. They can find that on the website.

Moneeka: Yay, thank you for that; that is so generous. Emma, it has been lovely having you on the show, thank you so much.

Emma: It has been my pleasure; thank you, Moneeka.

"Hands can build a house but hearts create a home."
~ UNKNOWN AUTHOR

BECOME THE LEADER YOU WERE MEANT TO BE
WITH MONEEKA SAWYER

Brrrrr . . . the cold air in the wee hours of Monday morning sent shivers up my spine. I rolled to my side and snuggled deep into my pillow. Fifteen minutes later, my alarm clock rang. Bzz! Bzz! Bzz! Holy cow! That's loud! Drowsily, I flung my arm out and whacked the snooze button. A few minutes later, the alarm clock rang again. I opened one eye and peered into the morning light. It took a minute or two for me to turn the alarm off and get out of bed, but get out of bed I did . . . and straight into a hot shower.

All dressed up and ready to go, I hustled down the stairs and brewed up some coffee, my first of the day. Ahh . . . so good! I curled my toes and rocked forward onto the balls of my feet. As soon as my heels touched the floor again, I was moving. With a granola bar clamped between my teeth, I slid into my jacket, swung my purse over my shoulder, grabbed my keys, and dashed out the front door. Twenty minutes later I was at the county planning department to negotiate the plans for my new building. I stood in front of a long, narrow table surrounded by middle-aged men in power suits and sour faces. I took a deep conscious breath, smiled brightly, and began . . .

Do you think you are not a leader type?
Do you want to be a leader?
When you take on a leadership role, do you feel like a fraud?

Have you ever found yourself confronted with addressing the most pressing issues of a day in front of an adversarial group of people? This is what leaders are often called to do! And yet, they are still composed enough to do this with grace and influence. But how? What is it about leaders that gives them the confidence and power to address a boardroom as easily as you might address a birthday party?

If you really want to know, then keep reading. Within the next few pages, I will tell you how you can connect with your own innate power and use it to create the ideal environment to accomplish your dreams. So hold on tight and let's get started!

When I was a little girl, I used to stand on the sidelines during recess and look out onto the vast playground, where children of all sizes and shapes were engaged in play. I would pay particular attention to the children who seemed to be the leaders in their play groups. They seemed confident and popular and, most importantly, happy. Standing under the darkness of the awnings alongside the school building, I decided that I would be one of them someday. But how would I overcome my shyness and cross the cultural barrier that always seemed to stand between them and me?

It wasn't until high school that I came to a turning point. I was going to a school dance, and I really wanted to fit in. So I put a lot of effort in dressing up and then drove off into adventure. When I got there, I entered the gym with flare. I had fantasized that I would be the prettiest, most desirable girl in the room and that all the boys I liked would forget their dates and make a beeline straight for me! But my fantasy remained just that—a fantasy. In reality, I ended up standing on the sidelines and looking on as others chatted and took to the dance floor. That night, I decided that I would stop looking to others for validation.

From then on, the disappointments didn't hurt as much, and my sense of isolation started to fade. I began to delve into the field of psychology to understand why I didn't fit in—and how I could change. I read book after book, experimenting from time to time with some of the strategies that I had learned.

Over the years, I have learned that leaders come in different forms and have many faces. I began to divide them into seven distinct groups and assigned each group a color. The chart below describes what I came up with.

RED	Those who are the pillars of society. They are solid, reliable, and stable.	George Washington Bill Gates Eleanor Roosevelt
ORANGE	Those who lead with creativity, playfulness, and joy.	Ellen Degeneres Princess Diana
YELLOW	Those who are powerful, confident, and inspire awe.	Oprah Winfrey Jean Luc Picard Margaret Thatcher
GREEN	Those who lead with connection, collaboration, and compassion.	Mother Teresa Nelson Mandela
BLUE	Those who lead with their words.	John F. Kennedy Dr. Martin Luther King, Jr. Susan B. Anthony
INDIGO/ NAVY BLUE	Those who lead with knowledge.	Ruth Bader Ginsburg Marie Curie Thomas Edison
WHITE	Those who lead by showing us how to elevate our spirit.	Mahatma Gandhi Maya Angelou

Each of the examples that I have listed have a combination of leadership styles. I have simply aligned them with their dominant style and corresponding color. The same goes for each of us. We all have a way that we prefer to be in the world, and this is the way that we are most comfortable being when we are in a leadership role.

You all know that you are all leaders, right? You know that you were born to lead. But did you know that you have a leadership ecosystem in your body? Your mind, your emotions, and your physiology are all part of this ecosystem. And the most important part of this ecosystem is your energy system.

Think of your ecosystem as a house. There are a lot of things that make that house what it is. Its structure. Its aesthetic. Its decor. All the conveniences inside. It may have gorgeous flooring, plush carpets, top-notch appliances, a beautiful garden, but what happens when the power goes out? How comfortable is it then? How functional is it? A house without electricity still serves the purpose of a house, but it isn't a blissful home. It isn't functioning at 100%. The same goes for the energy system in your body, what I call the Pillar of Perfection. Everything can be in good working order, but without the necessary energy, it is lifeless.

This energy system is our chakra system. Chakras are powerful energy centers that affect the physical, mental, and emotional well-being of the physical body. There are seven major chakras in the human energy body, and they are arranged vertically along the spine, starting at the base and moving up through the top of the head.

As shown in the chart below, each chakra has a specific name and a corresponding color associated with it. In addition, each chakra has a specific sound signature. For instance, the sacral chakra, the one located just below your belly button, corresponds to the color orange and the sound vaam.

CHAKRAS: Energy Centers in the energy body

NAME	COLOR	LOCATION	SOUND
Root	Red	Base of spine	*Laam*
Sacral	Orange	Lower abdomen, below the navel	*Vaam*
Solar Plexus	Yellow	Upper abdomen, above the navel	*Raam*
Heart	Green	Center of the chest	*Yaam*
Throat	Blue	Base of the throat	*Ham*
Third Eye	Indigo/Navy Blue	Lower forehead, between the eyebrows	*Au*
Crown	White	Just above the top of the head	*Mmm*

In your energy system, each chakra governs a particular area of your life. If it is blocked, that area will not function at its best. And because the chakras are all part of your Pillar of Perfection, each one affects all the others and nothing will work at its best.

So, it's important that we keep all our energy centers open and unblocked. And if all these centers are open, then together they can support us in being the most powerful leaders we can be in our preferred color styles.

Take a look at the two charts I presented above. What do you notice? There are seven main chakras, and each one of them corresponds to one of the colors of leadership. These seven chakras are the building blocks of your Pillar of Perfection. Once these centers are clear and your pillar of perfection is strong, everything else works more smoothly, and you are able to fully stand in your own natural, innate power. You are fully able to step forward as a leader in your own unique way.

Would you like to learn how to strengthen your Pillar of Perfection?

Remember, true leadership starts from the inside out.

If you open up your chakras, you will attract everything you want in your life. You will command respect, stand in your power, and be seen as an authentic leader. If you are not able to be your most powerful authentic self, people will subconsciously be able to tell. They may intellectually think of you as a leader, but they may not want to follow you. Or if they do follow, they may not stay long. A true leader must be true to herself in order to be able to lead long term. That's why you must focus on what is going on inside of you, at the deepest level first.

Keep in mind that it is very important to clear all the chakras because if you just clear one, it will get muddled up quickly by the unclear energies of the other chakras. But we have to start somewhere, and for us women, the best place to start is in the Sacral Chakra. This is our feminine power center. It is located a couple inches below your belly button.

This is our place of creation. From this place we give birth. We give birth to children. We give birth to ideas. We give birth to businesses. This is also a place of creativity, playfulness, and joy. This is the chakra that enhances the feminine power of attraction. The feminine attracts and receives, while the masculine pursues and provides.

Would you like to have a little taste of what it's like to clear your sacral chakra? Awesome. To create the Pillar of Perfection we focus on three things: breath, sound, and visualization.

Let's start with breath.

Close your eyes and take in a slow deep breath through your nose. Notice how far down the breath goes. Does it stop in your chest, or maybe even your throat?

Now release it slowly through your mouth.

You're going to take another deep breath in, but this time imagine that breath goes all the way down to tickle the back of your belly button.

Hold that breath for a moment, and then release it slowly through your mouth.

Practice this a bit. Each time you breathe in, imagine that you are breathing in bright white clean air into your body.

When you're ready, take a long, slow, deep breath of bright white air in through your nose to a count of 8. Imagine that breath goes all the way down to the back of your belly button.

Then hold the breath for a count of 4.

Then release the breath slowly through your mouth to a count of 8.

This breath energizes your entire body and helps to wash away those things that are blocking your chakras.

Next let's focus on sound.

The sound for the Sacral Chakra is Vaam.

Take your deep breath in to a count of 8, hold it for a count of 4, and as you release it to a count of 8, chant the word Vaaaaaaaaaaaaaaaaaaaaaam in one smooth breath.

Now let's add in the visualization.

The color of the Sacral Chakra is Orange.

Take your deep breath in to a count of 8, and hold it for a count of 4.

As you are holding this breath for a count of four, imagine a closed orange rosebud appearing in your Sacral Chakra.

As you release it, chant the word Vaaaaaaaaaaaaaaaaaaaaam in one smooth breath and imagine that orange rosebud opening up into a gorgeous orange rose in full bloom.

Just feel how your body relaxes and melts into the beauty of this chakra.

Do this same exercise for each of your chakras.

Use the chakra chart to guide you through this process.

Now that your chakras are more clear, let's take an honest look at what your natural leadership style is.

Leadership through any one of the chakras is wonderful, as long as all the chakras are balanced. If any of them are unbalanced, you may see the more negative consequences of your leadership style.

For instance, I lead through my Sacral Chakra. My brand is all about Bliss, which is about joy, playfulness, creativity, and experiencing all that life has to give. If you were to meet me, you would probably be surprised at how joyful I am. And I hope you would be inspired to create the same bliss for your own life. This works because I keep all my chakras clear and bright.

If someone were to lead through this chakra and not have a clean Pillar of Perfection, they might start leading with their sexuality. They may become manipulative and try to seduce, literally or figuratively, people into following them. Leading with your sexuality is not necessarily bad, as long as it is done with good intentions and in a way that respects others. However, if your chakras are not clear, you are much more likely to lead with your sexuality in a negative and even offensive way.

Leading through connection.

One of the most beautiful aspects of clearing your pillar of perfection is that it helps you to connect in a truly deep way with others. After all, isn't leadership about connecting with, inspiring, and leading others?

I'd like to teach you a simple technique to help you connect magically with someone. You can use a similar technique to connect with larger groups, too, but let's start by focusing on individual connections.

One thing to keep in mind is that as you connect with people using your energy, they will be reacting to what is going on inside of you. This happens naturally and unconsciously with all of us anyway, but now the response will be more dramatic because your energy is so much more powerful.

Can you imagine sending mucky energy out to someone? This actually happens all the time. Have you ever been in a really good mood and then chatted with someone and felt really irritated, distracted, or impatient afterward? That's because you picked up the energy they were radiating out. When you are connecting with people, you don't want to be sending out this kind of bad energy, right? You want to make sure when you do this connection exercise, you are balanced and strong and have good energy to share. You are going to connect heart-to-heart with people. Make sure your intentions are loving, or the connection can have unexpected negative results.

How to connect energetically with others.
Here is what you do.
1. First let's clear the Heart Chakra.
2. Take a couple breaths of bright white air in and out, and see the beautiful green rose open up and fill your Heart Chakra with light.
3. Now as you breathe in, imagine that air being infused with your loving, powerful Heart Chakra energy.
4. When you breathe out, imagine sending that breath like a bridge from your heart to the other person's heart.
5. Do this slowly and gently. Bridge the energy of your heart with the energy of theirs. Fill their heart with the loving energy you want to share.

Notice what happens. Often, the other person will visibly relax. They will start to smile. Sometimes even their voice will get a bit higher. It's so much fun to watch them react to our powerful, loving energy.

Isn't that amazing? Start practicing this in every single one-on-one interaction you have. See how your communications change. See how people respond to you differently. And watch how this becomes easier and easier.

Leadership at its most basic is about impacting other people. Through this exercise, you are able to impact someone in the most positive, loving way possible. And you can expand that impact one person at a time.

Be the authentic leader you were meant to be.

You are a natural leader. Understand what your leadership style is and allow yourself to lead in that way. Keep it unique to you.

Allow your most powerful, loving self to connect with those around you, and you will see how easily and magically you can be the leader you always wanted to be.

* * * *

As I looked around the table and noticed all the sour faces, I did what I do best. I smiled my most charming smile, sent my heart energy into the room, and began.

"Well, hello there, everyone! Shall we get started?"

This meeting was set because my partners and I were trying to build a condominium complex and had not been able to get our plans approved from the planning department. The conversation started heatedly, with each man arguing his case.

When it came to me, I said calmly, "You know, we are actually all on the same team. We all want Los Altos to stay beautiful, and we all want something beautiful to go into that empty property so that all the crime currently going on there stops. Handling this will save the city a lot of money in police surveillance as well as meeting everyone's needs."

The men all looked at me dumbstruck. After a pregnant pause, their expressions began to change. I controlled the conversation for the rest of the meeting, and one by one, they started nodding their heads. The aspiration of bettering their own community seemed to allay their fears and soften their resolves. I released the breath that I didn't know I had been holding and began to relax. Hope had resurfaced and a solution was in sight!

By the end of our time together, we had a plan in place that we all agreed on and a signed commitment by the planning department controller to approve it.

And VOILA! Sacral Chakra leadership at its best!

Imagine what you could do if you allowed yourself to be the leader you were meant to be. How would your life and your real estate business be different? How much more successful and gratifying would your negotiations be? Imagine how much more blissful wealth you could create.

> **"Always remember, goals without action are just dreams.**
> **Leaders take action. So go out there, take action, and**
> **create the life your heart deeply desires!"**
> **~MONEEKA SAWYER**

ABOUT MONEEKA SAWYER

Moneeka Sawyer is the Blissful Millionaire. She is often described as one of the most blissful people you will ever meet. But don't confuse her big smile and infectious laugh with naiveté. Her multi-million dollar real estate empire is just one example of her ability to strategize, organize, and implement big business plans.

She has been investing in real estate for over 20 years, so has worked through several different cycles of the market. Through her strategies, she has turned $10,000 into over $2,000,000, working only 5-10 hours per MONTH with very little stress.

She lives her dreams and won't let anyone tell her what she can and can't do. Even though she was constantly told she couldn't get in, she graduated from Haas Business School at UC Berkeley, one of the top 3 business schools in the nation. She has been in business for herself ever since. While building her multi-million dollar business, she has travelled to over 55 countries, dances every single day, and spends lots of time with her husband of over 25 years and her adorable little puppy (who is the love of her life, but shhhh...don't tell her husband).

Moneeka is the best-selling author of the book "Choose Bliss: The Power and Practice of Joy and Contentment," which was honored with the very prestigious Woman of Impact Quill Award by Focus on Women Magazine, the Pinnacle Book Achievement Award, and the Award for Best Literary Work from the Governor of the State of Maryland.

Her second book "Your Amazing Itty Bitty Blissful Real Estate Investing Book:15 Steps to Building Massive Wealth on Your Terms," is also a national bestseller.

Moneeka is the host of the radio show and podcast Real Estate Investing for Women where she focuses on all aspects of real estate investing including strategies, mindset, emotional mastery, money smarts, and so much more, to ensure her listeners' blissful success.

Her expertise, and bliss-filled laugh, have been featured on stages with Suzanne Sommers, Martha Stewart, and Hal Elrod at places like the Nasdaq Marketplace, the Harvard Club of Boston, and Carnegie Hall, and on TV on NBC, CBS, ABC, and Fox reaching over 150 million people.

To learn more about Moneeka and how you too can build wealth blissfully, go to www.Blissfulinvestor.com

A SPECIAL INVITATION

Thank you so much for spending time with me in this book. I'd love the opportunity to spend time with you in other ways. If you'd like to find out different ways that I can support you, please go to

www.BlissfulInvestor.com

There you will find out about my radio show, home-study courses, and upcoming events.

Because you are now part of my family, you get very nice discounts on anything you decide to participate in. So whenever you purchase and are asked for a **discount code**, please use:

REIFW2020BOOK

I'm looking forward to helping you even more to build your wealth blissfully with real estate!

Blissfully yours,
Moneeka Sawyer

YOUR OPINION CAN CHANGE LIVES!

Don't you agree that it is important for women to help each other rise and succeed blissfully? When a woman looks up "real estate" online, about a million books pop up. How does she know which one is best for her? Often, by reading the reviews. If you liked this book, and would like to help more women live more blissful, wealthy, independent lives, please help them by reviewing this book. A rising tide lifts all boats. Let's be the rising tide for all of us women. **Review this book NOW** and make a difference to so many lives.

www.ingramcontent.com/pod-product-compliance
Lightning Source LLC
Chambersburg PA
CBHW030510210326
41597CB00013B/852